Aristotle
DE ANIMA

The Focus Philosophical Library

ARISTOTLE
DE ANIMA

**Translated, with
Introduction and Notes**

Mark Shiffman

focus an imprint of
Hackett Publishing Company, Inc.
Indianapolis/Cambridge

Aristotle
De Anima
© 2011 Mark Shiffman

Previously published by Focus Publishing/ R. Pullins Company

Focus an imprint of
Hackett Publishing Company, Inc.
P.O. Box 44937
Indianapolis, Indiana 46244-0937

www.hackettpublishing.com

Cover illustration © David Graves, www.davidgraves.cc

ISBN-13: 978-1-58510-248-8

CONTENTS

On the Translation

The freshness and thought-stimulating power of Aristotle's Greek has been filtered and diluted over centuries by translation into Latin, by the conventions of medieval scholastic debate, and by the adaptation of this Latinate tradition to modern philosophical and academic uses by scholars at Oxford, Cambridge and Chicago. While far from thinking that all this amounts to a corruption of Aristotle, I have attempted to recover, as much as possible, what I understand to be the immediate rhetorical impact and associations of ideas Aristotle has tried to bring to bear in his innovative philosophical Greek. In this I have been inspired by the outstanding translations by Joe Sachs. While I have benefited from Sachs' exemplary fidelity to the text, I have not insisted, as Sachs does, on maintaining Aristotle's sometimes extraordinarily long sentences intact, since I do not think that the English language has the kind of resources that enable Greek to maintain clarity amid such extended complexity. I hope that what results from my efforts is the most literal, readable and jargon-free translation into English available.

Whenever I have thought it possible, I have tried to reproduce in my English the ambiguities that I have found in Aristotle's Greek. A lucid formulation that is easier to pin down than Aristotle's may satisfy a desire for clarity shared by the translator and the reader; but puzzling over the meaning of the text does more to render our thought active and open to what Aristotle may be saying. In some cases, however, when there is a range of possible translations leading to different meanings that cannot be corralled together in English, I have naturally had to make choices based on my interpretation of Aristotle's thought. I have sometimes (though very rarely) supplied words left out but implied by Aristotle when I thought that leaving them out in English would make a sentence utterly obscure. On the two occasions on which I have made my own conjectures about what the Greek text ought to be, I have presented my rationale in the footnotes.

This is (as far as I am aware) the first English translation based on the now authoritative Greek text edited by the French classicist Jannone. I have profited enormously from the thorough and judicious commentary by Ronald Polansky (*Aristotle's **De Anima**, Cambridge University Press,

2007), though I have not always followed his interpretations or textual construal of particular passages.

I have usually left the Greek word "*logos*" untranslated, except where it clearly refers strictly to a mathematical ratio or to a specific written discourse. I discuss the range of its meanings in the Glossary.

I am very much indebted to Keith Whitaker for inviting me to undertake this translation for Focus, and to Ron Pullins for publishing it and for extending me the benefit of his nearly endless patience. David C. Schindler generously read the whole translated text and offered helpful comments, and Jesse Couenhoven and Christopher Mirus provided valuable criticism of my introduction; Rebecca Goldner, Brian Satterfield, Kevin Hughes, and Marjolein Oele discussed some final details that were troubling me; and Sara Brill read the whole penultimate draft. Where I have had the wisdom to follow the advice of these judicious colleagues, the final product was the better for it. I am also grateful to all my students (especially Keenan Lynch, Ben Raymond and Kevin Ryan), colleagues, friends and relatives whose encouragement and enthusiasm for this project helped me see it through, and above all my wife Cristina, who has put up with the ever-increasing clutter in the study.

Introduction

1. What is Soul?

A contemporary reader opening up a book about the soul will probably be surprised to find a work of what might best be described as biology. Examining the reasons for such surprise may reveal some very questionable suppositions we moderns tend to bring to any discussion of "the soul" as well as some very questionable suppositions about the character of biological knowledge. We must try to become aware of these suppositions, and so prepared to question them. Only then can we be in a position to judge whether Aristotle presents us with an alternative understanding of soul that deserves to be taken seriously, or whether his thought on this topic should be treated as a mere historical curiosity.

We probably tend to think that biology examines the workings of bodies, and that "soul" means something "spiritual" rather than material. We may very well also think that questions about the soul belong to religion, whereas biology is a science. Typically, the signs one will point to as evidence of such a spiritual entity inhabiting the human body are consciousness and free will. And possibly we also believe that bodies are undeniably real, whereas there is room for dispute concerning whether what we call "soul" really exists or not. Aristotle offers an account of soul that does not begin from such assumptions.

According to Aristotle, an account is superior if it makes more sense than rival accounts. But "making more sense" involves three different aspects. First, it is simply more coherent in itself, less plagued with self-contradictory claims or conceptions. Second, it makes better and more complete sense of the phenomena it is supposed to explain. Third, it also makes clear what it is about the phenomena that would lead one to find those deficient alternative accounts plausible, and why those accounts miss something important: it is not enough to understand the weaknesses of rejected alternatives, but is necessary as well to understand how they are partial glimpses of truth, and why they are only partial. The aim of thoughtful examination is to make sense of our experience of things; and

3

our efforts to understand them and the mistakes we make along the way are inseparably part of that experience. Ultimately, however, the measure of the adequacy of those efforts of understanding is the extent to which they intelligently elucidate the full richness of the phenomena.

In the case of soul, the phenomena we must examine are living beings. Right away, we encounter a chasm between the suppositions noted above and the way Aristotle and his predecessors thought about living beings. We think it sensible to ask: "Does the living being we are considering have a soul or not?" We may think we can dispense with the idea of a soul if we can account for all observable aspects of a living being in terms of material processes. Aristotle did not think this. But what is more surprising is that even the most materialist philosophers who came before him did not think this. They thought that they were explaining soul in material terms, not eliminating it by materialistic explanation.

This divergence between ancient and modern materialists suggests that it is not simply because of its reduction of phenomena to material explanations that modern biology tends to ignore or set aside soul. Two possible explanations for this modern peculiarity immediately suggest themselves. One possibility is that there is a particular feature of modern materialism by which it differs from ancient versions, and that this difference must be responsible for the different treatment of soul. The other possibility is that the meaning of soul itself has changed. Or (as indeed seems to be the case) maybe both of these have occurred, and are related.

Let us consider first the difference between ancient and modern materialist biology. Unlike ancient materialism, modern materialist science generally accepts as evidence only what can be measured. One reason for this is institutional. Science is understood as a widespread collaborative research effort, and "scientific results" are those that can be verified by other researchers. But verification is most typically understood in terms of exactly reproducing the same or equivalent conditions and processes and ending up with the same or equivalent results. This experimental uniformity can only be achieved if the conditions admit of exact measurement. Thus verifiable research is limited to what can be measured. "Insight" is not reproducible this way, and so is not the essence of scientific knowledge, though it may assist the advancement of theories and procedures. "Insight" is much closer, however, to what Aristotle means by *theoria* (see Glossary, "Contemplation").

One reason the institutions of research have taken such a shape, however, is that they have usually been guided by an understanding of material being that differs from Aristotle's. That understanding is best articulated by Descartes: "Extension in length, breadth and depth constitutes the nature of corporeal substance; and thought constitutes the nature of thinking substance. Everything else which can be attributed to body presupposes extension, and is merely a mode of an extended thing; and similarly, whatever we find in the mind is simply one of the various modes of thinking."[1] What we most unavoidably know about the world of "external" experience is that it is extended or "spatial", and therefore quantifiable and measurable; and we distinguish this external world from the knower who stands over against it as a different kind of being.

Aristotle has a different account of perception and knowledge of things in the world, and we will return to this shortly. For the moment, what is important to see is that Descartes' conception (based on a method of thinking that seeks to begin with what is most certain, clear and distinct to us) divides the world of our experience into "matter" (external and quantifiable or objectifiable) and "spirit" or "mind" (internal and "subjective"). "Spirit" in this sense is not equivalent to what Aristotle means by "soul," and "matter" in this sense is not equivalent to what Aristotle means by "material" (see Glossary, "Material").

It is this Cartesian conception, or something like it, that underlies the prevalent assumption that science (including biology) examines matter, whereas soul (in the sense of "spirit") belongs to non-scientific thought—perhaps philosophy, but above all religion. Psychology—study of *psuche* or soul—in modern times finds itself vacillating between these polarities, in some cases restricting itself to quantifiable bodily motions (whether "behaviors" or neural processes), in some cases examining forms of consciousness as they are revealed in speech, and sometimes trying to strike a middle path.

Because modern scientific biology generally treats living beings in terms of the quantifiable processes peculiar to them, it has a strong tendency to look at them as machines. The great problem in modern science is to understand how life can originate from mechanistic, non-living matter. As the philosopher of biology Hans Jonas has pointed out, the nearly universal and natural human experience of the world (before it is reshaped by modern physics, chemistry and biology) is that everything is alive.[2] Post-Cartesian thought, by removing spirit from external beings and looking upon everything external as dead, gives rise to a conception of soul's presence in things that has been described as "the ghost in the machine." Thus on this view, the question of whether soul is a necessary concept for describing reality comes down to the question whether we think the machine of the body needs a ghost to "animate" it.

---

1   Descartes, *Principles of Philosophy*, Part 1, Principle 53, in *The Philosophical Writings of Descartes, Volume I* (Cambridge University Press, 1985)

2   Jonas, "Life, Death, and the Body in the Theory of Being," in *The Phenomenon of Life: Toward a Philosophical Biology* (Northwestern University Press, 2001)

As we have seen, the ancient materialists saw the problem differently. They did not think of soul in terms of a "concept" that was added by the mind to the experience of living things, but as an observable aspect of the phenomena. Living things differ noticeably from non-living things. "Soul" refers to whatever is responsible for that difference. On this understanding of "soul" it makes no sense to ask whether any particular living thing has a soul or not, but only to ask what that soul really is. Anyone who has cared for a plant knows that vitality is observable. A question one could raise, and that Aristotle does raise in the first chapter, is whether soul is separable from body. (Again, since we tend to think of soul in terms of "spirit," we may tend to assume that separateness from the body is already part of the concept of soul.)

How do living things differ from non-living? As Aristotle observes in the second chapter of Book One, most people who have considered the question have typically pointed to two prominent features of ensouled beings: they move themselves and they perceive. These criteria already raise a difficulty if we understand soul as the principle of life. Plants clearly have life, but do not clearly perceive. They do, however, move themselves in a certain sense, by growing, blossoming, and so on. As Aristotle notes, the tendency to emphasize these two criteria reflects an emphasis on animal life and inattention to the life of plants. As we shall see, when Aristotle chooses his own starting point at the beginning of Book Two, he remedies this deficiency.

While the emphasis on perception and self-motion is a bit skewed, it is not entirely unreasonable, since these are the most striking features of living things, the ones that most readily set them apart at first glance. These marks that most of Aristotle's predecessors relied upon, in fact, may well remind us of the ones we tend to associate with soul. Perception, as meant by his predecessors, has about the same range as what we call "consciousness" or "mind" (see Glossary under "Intellect" and "Perception"). Self-motion also seems to bear some resemblance to free will and choice. The differences, however, reflect different understandings of soul at work. Perception implies something perceived, a relationship between the soul and things in the world; consciousness belongs to the conscious subject, the "spirit," and raises the question whether it corresponds to anything "outside." Likewise, self-motion is something we observe in a bodily being, whereas "free will" suggests a largely spiritual and interior phenomenon.

As a result, Aristotle's *On the Soul* both is and is not about the things we might expect. It does turn out to be about the sense in which soul is incorporeal, but it articulates the non-bodily character of soul in terms of the intrinsically related principles of material and form, rather than in terms of the dualistically opposed principles matter and spirit. It does raise what we might consider a religious question about whether the soul is immortal or not, but treats this as somewhat tangential to the main line of inquiry, secondary to the question of what soul is. It does treat of what we call "consciousness," but does not assume that our starting point must be our own inner world split off from the outer; and it argues for the necessity of clear distinctions between perception, imagination and thought. Finally, by investigating self-motion, it arguably gets closer to the heart of the question of freedom than it is possible to get by starting out from a supposed spiritual faculty of free will. In all of these respects, it challenges modern formulations of the problem of soul, and requires us to think more critically about what exactly is at issue.

Having given some initial clarification of the different perspective Aristotle opens for us on the being of soul, we are better prepared to consider how he unfolds his examination.

2. How to Investigate Soul?

On the Soul both is and is not like a Socratic dialogue. It does not present us with the drama of Socrates posing vexing questions to other characters who have something at stake in the answers they give. It does, however, incorporate three vital features of the kind of dialogic inquiry exemplified by Socrates. Aristotle motivates inquiry by arousing perplexity; he engages in a kind of dialogue with earlier thinkers who have discoursed about soul; and he gives priority to the guiding question of what the thing under discussion really *is*. Attention to these three features brings to light how they serve as orienting threads to Aristotle's inquiry.

Perplexity. In Plato's *Meno*, Socrates is famously compared (at 80a) to a stingray who stupefies his victims. The odd thing is that, after being subjected to questioning by Socrates, one suddenly knows less than one thought one knew. This disorienting experience provides the orientation for raising the formerly unasked questions about what one thought was known.

This experience of perplexity is described in Greek as "*aporia*" or "lack of resource." A *poros* is, in its most concrete meaning, a bridge or ford across a stream. In "a-poria" one is pulled up short and has no clear way to go forward (thus Joe Sachs typically translates it "impasse"). Sometimes perplexity results from getting oneself into a muddle of thought. It can also, however, result from difficulties inherent to what one is thinking about.

In the first chapter of Book III of his *Metaphysics*, Aristotle offers a striking explanation of the importance of beginning an inquiry with carefully delineated aporiai; and in the rest of Book III he meticulously develops the perplexities involved in understanding what it is to be a being.

This reflection on the relevant aporiai comes after his discussion (in Book I) of the teachings of his predecessors about the first principles of being and intelligibility.

In *On the Soul* Aristotle does the reverse. After a first paragraph about the importance of investigation of soul, he launches straight into articulation of the perplexities involved, and only subsequently examines the teachings of his predecessors. In each text, the order is appropriate to the inquiry. The real perplexities about the first principles of being and intelligibility only come into view after poets and philosophers have made initial efforts to articulate such principles and the inquirer has attempted to see the world in terms of the various principles articulated. The perplexities concerning soul are more immediately available to us, for in some way human beings naturally come to face questions about the relationship of body and soul —especially when faced with the problem of mortality and of their kinship with and difference from the other animals.

In Book I, chapter 1, Aristotle elaborates twelve perplexities:

1. How should one pursue the inquiry in the first place—with what manner of proceeding and from what starting points?

2. What kind of being is soul in terms of the categories of being he has elsewhere distinguished (see Glossary, "Categories")?

3. Does it exist as potential or as fully itself (see Glossary, "Potential" and "Being-fully-itself")?

4. Is it divisible into parts?

5. Are all souls (especially of different kinds of living things) the same in kind or different?

6. If different, are they different at every level of specification, or are there groups of living things which have fundamentally the same kind of soul within their grouping and differ as such from other groupings?

7. Is there a single *logos* (see Glossary, "Logos") for all soul as such?

8. If there are parts of soul, do we begin examining it from the whole or from the parts?

9. If there are parts, what are their natural differences?

10. If examining parts, do we start from the parts themselves or from their characteristic works?

11. If examining works, do we start from the works themselves or from the things to which they are oriented?

12. How fundamentally and integrally connected are body and soul?

Most of these perplexities attain some kind of resolution (or if not resolution, then sharpening of the question and clarification of what a resolution would require) in the first four chapters of Book II. Perplexity 9 (the natural differences of parts) attains its fullest clarification in III.9. Perplexity 6 cannot be resolved within a general examination of soul, since it requires more detailed and extended investigation of the kinds of living things; the investigation of soul can, however, clarify what one must look for in such examinations in order to address this perplexity. The treatments of perplexities 1, 8, and 12 call for a few more extended observations.

The first perplexity, as Aristotle also states it, is whether there is a single way to approach all questions of what something is. After articulating the first eleven perplexities, Aristotle pauses to reflect upon this first one, and suggests that it requires not a choice between alternative ways of proceeding, but rather a circularly reinforcing combination of them: Not only does understanding what a thing is make its distinctive attributes more intelligible, "but also the attributes in turn contribute a great deal toward understanding what it is" (402b18-403a2). This enriching and deepening circularity is characteristic of what Plato called dialectical thinking.

Aristotle puts such enriching circularity to work in Books II and III, and explains in II.3 why he does so. In the first two chapters of Book II, he articulates a general account of what soul as such is, but then in II.3 explains why this cannot serve as a proper starting point for detailed inquiry into soul. What the attempt at a general account does show is that soul has to be understood in terms of the characteristic activities of different kinds of living beings. This, however, clearly entails that our investigation concern itself with those activities. Thus the resolution of perplexity 8, whether to start from the whole or the parts, is roughly as follows: Start from the whole to understand more clearly why you must start over again from the parts and their distinct activities (without ever forgetting the question of their unity and relationships in the whole).

Perplexity 12, concerning the inextricability of the body-soul relationship, clearly concerns the question of the separability of soul, and hence of the possibility of the soul's surviving the death of the body. Aristotle immediately proceeds to reflect on this perplexity in the remainder of I.1. Here he indicates already what a resolution of this perplexity requires: "[I]f one of the works or affections of the soul is peculiar to it, soul could be separate" (403a10). He already announces as well that intellect is, at first glance, the best candidate for an activity of soul that does not depend on embodiment. Thus, while the question of separability is implicitly at issue all the way through the investigations of Books II and III, it is not surprising that Aristotle returns explicitly to this question in III.4-8, the chapters investigating contemplative intellect. These chapters do not provide an unambiguous resolution. They do, however, clarify what such a resolution requires, namely an adequate understanding of: a) whether contemplative intellect is ultimately independent in some way of perception and imagination; b) how contemplative intellect is related to the intelligibles it contemplates; and c) how to understand properly the nature of and relationship between intellect as pure potentiality (or receptivity) and intellect as active (or productive of the intelligibility of what it contemplates).

Given these requirements, we can see that the digression that constitutes much of the remainder of I.1, on the question of the proper character of inquiry into nature, is after all not merely tangential to the question of the soul's separability. Aristotle concludes that digression thus: "The student of nature is concerned with all the works and affections of a certain sort of body and a certain sort of material, ... and the practitioner of first philosophy treats of separable things" (403b11-16). The question of the separability of contemplative intellect straddles biological psychology and first philosophy or metaphysics.[3] This is as true for us as it was for Aristotle. The three challenges listed above for resolving the question are still just as challenging; and it is still tempting to thinkers today (as it was for many of Aristotle's predecessors) to claim to have resolved the perplexity by sidestepping one or more of these challenges—most commonly today by asking us to believe that biological and psychological science can provide adequate answers in isolation from metaphysics.

Predecessors. Even though certain perplexities naturally arise for one who reflects on soul, at the same time one never starts from scratch. Others have come before us and have had something to say about soul. In I.2 Aristotle observes that reflecting upon what previous thinkers have said about soul helps us in two ways: "[W]e may take up what has been well said and be on guard against anything not well said" (403b23-24).

Everyone who arrives at reflective awareness does so within a community of speakers, and their speaking is laden with and passes along the thoughts of others on all matters of shared human experience. The thoughts embedded in speech are a mixture of insight and error. In order to disentangle insight and error, one must examine what is said with a view to rendering explicit and more highly visible the thought within it. This was always the initial aim of Socrates' questioning.

The intention of Socrates and of Aristotle is not, however, simply to sift out the insight and discard the error. What is "not well said" is not simply something to be set aside, but something to "guard against." We

---

3   Aristotle discusses the limited reach of natural investigation of soul when it comes to treat of intellect in his *Parts of Animals*, I.1, 641a33-b10. (I am grateful to Christopher Mirus for reminding me of this passage.)

are prone to certain kinds of errors when we think about something like soul. Some are natural and commonly recurring while others are factitious and merely part of our particular inheritance. Examining intently and thoughtfully what predecessors have said and bringing their words into higher focus helps us to see more clearly the errors to which we are prone and the limited conceptions we may take for granted. We have seen earlier that reflecting on a single passage from Descartes helps us bring into focus a conception of "matter"—as characterized primarily by spatial extension and as dualistically opposed to spirit—that is embedded in the whole way of thinking about knowledge and nature that we moderns inherit and that Descartes helped to shape. To take such an inherited conception for granted is to lack critical self-awareness as a thinker and to fall short of understanding fully the questions involved in reflecting on soul.

Aristotle's predecessors, as we have noted, tend to identify soul as the source of self-motion and of perception in living things. What almost all of them attempt to do is find some material basis for these characteristics. Those who think in terms of atoms ask what kinds of atoms would plausibly cause such characteristics, and those who think in terms of four or more basic elements identify one of them or some combination of them as constituting soul. The atomists tend to think that the smoothest and finest-grained atoms would be soul-atoms, while the elementalists identify every element but earth as plausible candidates. Aristotle notes that, in favoring such candidates, these thinkers also imply a third distinguishing characteristic that guides their thought about soul: They are all looking for something with a relatively incorporeal character (405b11-12). This involves their approach in a paradox that goes unnoticed, namely the attempt to arrive at a conception of the non-bodily by minimizing the bodily features of bodies. (Those who think of soul as spirit have a parallel tendency, for it is hard to imagine a spirit as anything other than a disembodied body-like thing.) This implicit goal of articulating the incorporeal character of soul points in the direction of the more adequate articulation Aristotle will give in Book Two: Soul is best understood as form rather than in terms of material.

Two other shortcomings of preceding thinkers point likewise toward understanding soul in terms of form. The first is that these material explanations try to account for the phenomena in terms of parts, and fail to say anything about how the presence of soul is related to the wholeness of a living thing. "The elements, at least, seem more like material, whereas that which holds a thing together, whatever it may be, is the most decisive factor.... Their conception of the soul as being in these elements seems to rest on the homogeneity of the whole with its parts" (410b11-12, 411a16-17). While a thing has soul, it continues to be the distinct whole that it is, and when soul "departs", what was a body of that kind of living thing then disintegrates back into elements.

The other shortcoming is that the focus on motion and perception tends to ignore plants, which are certainly living beings. The principle life-activity of plants is self-nourishment and growth, along with reproduction. This kind of life-activity is fundamental to all living bodies on earth: they are all unities engaged in sustaining their own unity, in attaining the fullness of their form in growth and maturation, and in propagating that form to be embodied in material other than their own. While the focus on motion and perception rightly points to understanding soul in terms of activity, it also indicates a failure to notice the less striking but more universal and fundamental activity of ensouled beings, which is maintaining and preserving their form. This characteristic of soul is fundamental for Aristotle's whole subsequent account. It is no coincidence, then, that Aristotle concludes his reflection on preceding thinkers and makes his transition to his "new beginning" that articulates soul as form with the following thought: "The governing principle in plants seems indeed to be some kind of soul, since this alone is shared by both plants and animals; and while it does exist separately from the perceptive principle, nothing has perception without this" (411b27-30). The activity of maintaining form (including developing to maturity under its guidance and propagating it) which plants exhibit is the key to understanding soul rightly.

What soul is. One of the inherited teachings about soul is, in certain respects, similar to the one Aristotle will go on to articulate. This is the notion "that soul is a certain harmony" (I.4). (Such a notion is defended by the Pythagorean character Simmias in Plato's *Phaedo*.) By making soul a property of bodily interactions rather than a distinct kind of body itself, this view both remains materialistic and at the same time grants soul a kind of incorporeality.

Aristotle observes that the main weakness of this view is that, by making soul derivative from body, it is unable to make any sense of the causal role soul seems to have in bodily life. The ratio of elements and relationship of parts in our body is the same the moment after we die as it was before, so how can the "harmony" suddenly be gone? Nevertheless, the harmony-view takes us a step closer to understanding soul as form, and to understanding this form as intimately related to the body it informs.

Carrying the musical analogy further may help to clarify what it means to speak of soul as a distinct being and as causal form. Consider Mozart's String Quartet number 16. It came into existence in Mozart's imagination, and he encoded it in musical notation. It has active existence (or "life") whenever four musicians get together and play it. It is not the musicians who make the quartet exist. Rather, it is the existence of the quartet as a form that governs the coordinated actions of the musicians. Any four capable musicians playing the relevant instruments can serve as the material foundation for the life of that piece of music, but only because the form of the music is already there to organize their movements.

Now consider a squirrel. Its life consists of certain activities, and to be alive as a squirrel means to have the capacities to engage in those activities. A squirrel that is not properly equipped for "squirreling" will not continue to be a squirrel for long. It needs the relevant parts, and for these parts to do their work it requires that they be composed of the suitable materials. Since the materials come and go, it is not, strictly speaking, the materials that are responsible for its being a squirrel. Rather, it is having the right kind of materials in the right arrangement. In accounting for the squirrel's being what it is, the form has priority over the material. But it has that form (teeth and claws and tail all shaped in particular ways and proportions) in order to do well the things it does as a squirrel; thus "form" ultimately refers to the complex of life-activities that constitute "squirreling." But since the squirrel continues to be a living squirrel although it can never perform fully and all at once all the activities that constitute its squirrel-hood, it is not the performance of the acts of squirreling, but rather maintaining the capacities for those acts that constitutes its continuing to be alive as a squirrel. It is in order to maintain these capacities that it incorporates the materials it needs into its body and sustains the parts it needs for those activities in a proper proportion to one another. Thus Aristotle says that soul is the "being-fully-itself" (*entelecheia*) of an organized living body, in the sense of its being fully capable of that living thing's proper activities and its sustaining itself in this form.

Thus we see why overlooking the life of plants leads to a failure to recognize what soul is. The primary and most universal manifestation of soul in a living thing is that this living thing matures toward the fullness of its capacities for a characteristic set of life-activities, and also maintains itself in that form. This is the work of what Aristotle calls the nutritive power (which is also sometimes called the vegetative power; and since it is the one power of living things that plants clearly have, they have come to be called vegetables). He also remarks that reproduction is a work of this same power: As nutritive, it brings to completeness the body that serves as its material foundation, and incorporates new material to maintain that completeness; as reproductive, it perpetuates that form in new material of the same kind. In both aspects, the basic work of soul is perpetuation of its complete form in appropriate material organized suitably.

It may be worth noting in passing that the discovery of DNA does not in any way undermine this account, but might even be understood as strengthening it. In the terms of the musical example, DNA corresponds to the musical notation; it encodes the form, or bears the "information" that enables bodily material to become "in-formed" and active in a particular way. Indeed, the Nobel Prize-winning biologist Max Delbruck once suggested that the Prize Committee "should consider Aristotle for the discovery of the principle implied in DNA."[4]

3. Perceiving and Discerning Beings

If, like Descartes, we start by supposing or imagining a radical distinction between matter (extension) and spirit (consciousness), we will encounter a difficulty in understanding the connection between the mind and the world. Do the contents of our consciousness correspond strictly, or even loosely, to anything real in the world? I see red; but because the primary characteristic of external being is its quantitative extension, I can only confidently say that what is out there corresponding to the redness I see is some set of quantitative spatial relations among bodies. Furthermore, it is not even clear (as Kant makes evident) that I can confidently say that. Perhaps spatiality itself is merely the form of my apprehension of the "external" and therefore is, as far as I know, only something "in me" that may not correspond in any strict way to what is "out there" in "the thing itself." The challenge of accounting for how we can bridge this gap, or of what we are entitled to say we know if we can't bridge this gap, gives rise to what comes to be called "epistemology" (a word invented in the nineteenth century).

In this sense, Aristotle does not have an epistemology, because he does not need one. The real being of a natural living body "out there" is not its quantitative spatial relations, but its form. Form in the primary sense means its self-sustained complex of potencies for its array of characteristic life-activities (in other words, its soul, or the governing principle of the living being that it continues to be). Form in this primary sense is responsible for its having the bodily structure it has, so as to have a body serving as the material cause or ground of these potencies and activities. Its bodily form or shape is responsible for its visible form (and sensible form more generally). Vision (and perception in general) is the receptivity to form without its material. Hence the form that appears in my senses gives me access to the form that is the very being of the living thing itself. Thus, though there is frequent error and deception, there is no fundamental chasm between the senses and the beings in the world. (An analogous account can be given for non-living natural bodies, as well as for artificial bodies.)

---

4   "Aristotle-totle-totle," p.55 (in Ernest Borek and Jacques Monod, *Of Microbes and Life*, Columbia University Press, 1971)

Perceiving as a form of being. To prepare us for his account of the recognition of beings, Aristotle looks back again at his predecessors. They tend to say that perception "is a case of like being affected by like" (II.5, 416b35). This leads them to give a materialistic account of perception. The same thing happens in modern materialist thought. If we follow the dualism of Descartes, we end up with things radically unlike, and no accounting for their relationship. In order to have a coherent account, we may try to evict the ghost from the machine, and account for perception purely materialistically as a process of particles affecting particles, which "is a case of like being affected by like."

But properly speaking, perception is the act of apprehending certain kinds of qualities (and the capacity for such acts of apprehension). This is its formally distinct being, which is quite distinguishable from its material basis, however dependent it may be on that material basis. Each perceptual sense is oriented toward its particular range of qualities, and this orientation governs the development of the organs whose activity is the kind of perception in question. Perception exists as potential for its characteristic being-at-work, which is the apprehension of perceptible form. The vision is potential for seeing red; the cardinal is at work being red, and brings the vision into the being-at-work of seeing red. Thus the perceptive power is initially unlike, and becomes like (417a20).

But in thus becoming like the object, which is what it is oriented to do, the sense becomes fully itself, or fulfills its characteristic form as the sense that it is. This requires us to understand "being acted upon" in a rather different way than we are accustomed to. If we think in terms of extended matter, being acted upon is being changed from one measurable state (position, frequency) to another. But if we think in terms of a thing's nature, being brought into full activity is "the preservation of what has being in potential by what has being as fully itself and is like it" (417b3-4). The sight, brought into its characteristic being-at-work by color, becomes fully what it is, or achieves and enacts its natural form. The activity of the sense becomes one with the activity of what is sensible. Both attain the fullness of their being in the act that unites them.

Thus, just as, by the nutritive power, the animal matures into being fully itself and actively sustains this form, so also the exercise of the senses is a way of being fully itself as a being capable of such sensing. Just as nutritive thriving is a kind of vitality and fulfillment of a distinct potential, so is the exercise and enjoyment of the senses (for their healthy exercise is pleasurable, just as thriving bodily health is). Aristotle's account of the soul consistently identifies it as the being of the living thing as form, and form as the sustained potential for the characteristic activities that fulfill the thing's distinct nature.

Perception and thought. As we have seen, Aristotle's predecessors do not tend to divide consciousness from the world of beings. They do, however, like Descartes, tend to identify perception and thinking, so that whether they speak of perception (*aisthesis*) or intellect (*nous*), the meaning usually extends to both the phenomena distinguished by these terms, and so might be translated in either case as "mind" or "consciousness" (but without the dualistic implications those bear after Descartes). Thus, when Aristotle concludes the account of perception and begins to pass on to intellect, he reminds us that "the ancients say that understanding and perceiving are the same thing" (III.3, 427a21). To clarify what intellect is, Aristotle "must investigate what distinctive difference it has, as well as how thinking ever comes about" (III.4, 429a10). How thinking comes about entangles it intimately with perception and imagination, so that one can understand how "the ancients" (or anyone else) would fail to recognize intellect's distinctive difference. Here again, Aristotle brings to view both the more satisfactory account and why we tend to miss it.

Perception and intellect are alike in that they are both powers of the soul that attain their fullness of being when they are brought into activity by their proper objects, and are united with these objects in such a way that the forms of things are present in the soul without their material. Thus, "as what is perceptive is related to the perceptibles, so must the intellect bear a similar relationship to the intelligibles" (III.4, 429a17-18). This seemingly simple formulation already implicitly contains the solution to the whole question. The two are alike by analogy; they are the same, yet different. After two chapters in which Aristotle examines the power of intellect to apprehend intelligibles as such (III.4-5), he will go on to consider how the intellect apprehends wholeness and unity together with division, sameness together with difference (III.6), and then how it renders things intelligible as a whole through its recognition of analogy, which is the very union of sameness and difference (III.7). Reflection on the analogy of perception and intellect, which involves their sameness and their difference, is at the same time the enactment of the intellect's distinctive difference: its ability to understand what things are, and the sameness and difference among the things that are.

But the analogy between the senses and intellect is mediated in crucial ways by two other intermediate powers: the "common sense faculty" and imagination. Before Aristotle passes from the senses to intellect, he has to tease out the distinct differences of these overlooked powers (in III.1-3). The chapter on intellect that treats of analogy (III.7) is primarily concerned to clarify the analogies among these four kinds of "consciousness" and in this way to provide an integrative account of them. Only after this is done can Aristotle safely speak summarily of perception and intellect in parallel terms (III.8).

Sensus communis and *phantasia*. Each sense recognizes qualities in its range: visibles, sounds, tangibles, flavors, odors. But in addition to these "proper sensibles" there are "common sensibles" which we also recognize: "the things called 'common' are motion, rest, number, shape and size, since such things are not proper to any one of them, but common to all" (II.6, 418a16-18). Aristotle initially justifies calling these sensibles "common" on the grounds that we apprehend them by way of each of the different senses. After discussing the various senses, he comes back to these common sensibles and adds the important observation that we relate the different kinds of sensible qualities to one another, especially when they come to us from the same entity. Accordingly, in addition to the common sensibles listed the first time round, he includes "unity" in the second list (III.2, 425a16). By virtue of relating a variety of proper sensibles to one another, we more adequately perceive the common sensibles, and especially the unity of the substantial beings to which the proper sensibles belong as qualities. (Modern neurological science confirms this role for sensory integration, and more accurately locates it materially in the central nervous system rather than, as Aristotle did, in the heart.)

It is, thus, what came to be called in the Latin Aristotelian tradition the *"sensus communis"* that first enables us to recognize the distinct unity of distinct beings. Even animals without reason can do this, distinguishing, for example, the different prey that require different hunting tactics. Humans can go further and give an accurate and intelligible account of what each substantial being distinctively is (as this book attempts to do more generally for soul). The common sense faculty plays an intimate role in this exercise of reason; and the intimacy of this involvement further explains why it is so easy to conflate perceiving and thinking.

In order to dispel more decisively the apparent sameness of sensing and thinking, Aristotle has to distinguish another previously overlooked faculty, that of imagining (III.3). Whereas the common sense faculty is really the ultimate seat of the act of perceiving, and thus is not a separate faculty distinct from perception, imagination (*phantasia*) arises from perception, but works in a very different way. Imagination is, simply put, "that through which some image comes about for us" (III.3, 428a1). It enables us to present images to ourselves. Aristotle is only concerned here with this mere presentational role, and not with questions about the retention and recall of images; these he investigates further in *On Memory and Recollection*. These latter faculties are in some sense modes of imagination, and all are ultimately derivative from the common faculty of sense (*On Memory and Recollection* 450a9-15).

This ability to make images be present to oneself in the absence of the things of which they are images is crucial to thinking, both for deliberative or practical intellect and for contemplative intellect. Deliberation requires that we hypothetically connect images sequentially to sketch out a possible course of action. Aristotle has early on, in considering how to go about inquiring into soul, given an indication of the role of imagination in contemplation: "when we are able to give an account of all or most of the attributes in accord with our mental image [phantasia], then we will also be able to speak most excellently about the distinct being" (I.1, 402b22-25). To understand something better is, in part, to progressively fine-tune the relationships of the being and its attributes as they stand in our imagination, bringing them into greater accord with the relationships that really exist in the beings themselves.

As imagination is crucial to gaining understanding of the distinct being and attributes of things, so also is it essential for recognizing analogy. Aristotle gives a practical illustration of this in III.7, when he asks us to think of items in a certain proportional relationship, and then to alter the positions of the terms (i.e. images) and consider what new relationship comes to light (431a14-b1). After putting us through this exercise, he observes: "So then it is in the images that the intellective power thinks the forms" (431b2). The analogy that we recognize is not exactly an image, but rather an intelligible relationship among images; the distinct intelligible being we contemplate is not exactly an image either, but is somehow the intelligible content of the image. Hence Aristotle concludes his contemplation of contemplative intellect by saying: "But in what respect will the primary thoughts differ from being images? These are not images, but are not present without images either" (III.8, 432a12-14).

Any animal with a perceptual system sufficiently diverse to have what can properly be called a common sense faculty relating different senses will almost certainly have imagination as well. Imagination, arising from the being-at-work of perception, may be always involved to some degree in the act of perception. The most reliable distinguishing mark between the two is that the senses apprehend what is present, while imagination presents images also of what is not present. While the sensus communis registers differences and relates perceived qualities to the unity of the being to which they belong, phantasia makes such recognitions available for thought to reflect actively upon at all times. This reflection apprehends intelligibles that go somehow beyond the mere images, but nonetheless are barely if at all separable from the images; and the results of this reflection enter into and inform our subsequent perceptions and imaginings. While careful reflection can distinguish these faculties, in our experience they remain intimately bound up together, and so are easily equated with one another.

The error of conflating thought and perception is perennial, common to both the materialism of Aristotle's predecessors and the idealism of Descartes and Kant that begins from "consciousness". But the terms of the conflation are different. Aristotle's predecessors, not having distinguished out the faculty of imagination, use either perception or thought as the comprehensive term. In either case, they still assume some connection of our awareness to the things of which we are aware. Descartes and Kant, thinking in the wake of the philosophical tradition that had incorporated Aristotle's insights, tend in effect to interpret all thinking and perceiving primarily as "consciousness", which is arguably to reduce both to imagination. Thus consciousness is primarily the presence in us of images with no immediate mooring to the things of which they are images (if in fact they are images of anything). Nietzsche's thought, in which we can trust neither the senses nor the intellect to tell us anything about the world, would seem to be a natural result of this development.

At the same time, by defining the intelligible being of the external world as *res extensa*, extension and its measurable magnitude, Descartes elevates Aristotle's "common sensibles" to primary status as the intelligible principles of material beings. For Aristotle, the common sensibles are secondary from both directions. They are characteristics belonging incidentally to bodily beings whose primary principles of being are form and the material in which form is realized. Nor are they the primary objects of sense perception, but always come along with the perceptions of the proper sensibles. While they necessarily accompany the bodies in which form is at work, and are directly implicated in perceptions of bodily things, the common sensibles are secondary and derivative in both cases.

Thus one might plausibly say that the key to the Cartesian revolution is that it turns Aristotle's psychology inside out. Imagination becomes the inner reality, the common sensibles become the outer reality, and perception and thought are thrown entirely into question as ways of recognizing beings. The one common sensible that retains no credibility after Descartes is unity: it is because of its form that a thing is a unity, so that if the apprehended form is cast entirely into doubt, so is the unity of the thing. Thus, in Richard Dawkins' Cartesian account of biology, an organism is no real unity, but a "colony of genes."[5] (The dissolution of unity into extension is expressed in Descartes' algebraic geometry, in which numbers are not "multitudes of units" as they were for the ancients, but expressions of relations between extended magnitudes, or locations on a "number line." Thanks to the place it has attained in our educational curricula, both in mathematics and in

---

5   Richard Dawkins, *The Selfish Gene* (Oxford University Press, 2006), p.46

the sciences, the Cartesian coordinate system has come to dominate the modern imagination of external reality.)

4. Self-motion and Freedom

I suggested at the beginning of this introduction that the question that we tend to pose in terms of free will might in some way correspond to the question Aristotle poses in terms of self-motion. For us, the most typical way for this question to arise is from the "ghost in the machine" problem. If we look at the external world in terms of measurable extension and quantitative relations, we will tend to see its operations as mechanical, since the quantitative relations seem to follow patterns of necessity that, in modern times, have been called "laws of nature." If our acts of choosing represent some gap in this mechanical account, then there is a need for a ghost in the machine; if we can explain every thought and act in mechanical terms, maybe we don't need such a ghost. We tend to assume (as Descartes seems to have been the first to do) that animals are simply complicated machines, and that humans, who experience themselves as making free choices, may or may not be the exception. Shall we hold on to the Cartesian dualism (perhaps in the more satisfactory articulation in terms of "nature" and "freedom" worked out by Kant), or shall we accept the tidier materialistic and mechanistic explanation of our being (which rejects the experience of free choice as merely "subjective" or "epiphenomenal")? Do our actions issue from "us" or from the mechanical effects of material structures and forces?

As we have seen, for Aristotle the world of nature is not an external realm of mathematical necessity opposed to an inner realm of spirit and freedom. As he explains in *Physics* II.1, for something to have a nature is for it to be guided by an internal principle of motion and rest (192b21-23). This nature of the thing is properly its form; in living things, at least, it is the form that guides the development from inside (193b6-8). *On the Soul* makes clear that, for living things, that formal principle is what we mean by soul. To be alive is to be continually oriented toward and engaged in sustaining, enacting and fulfilling that form in its suitable material. Whereas modern dualism attempts to locate soul as a non-mechanical point of origin for a mechanical process (because it conceives of the self as spirit), Aristotle has a different understanding of the self in "self-motion" and of how it originates motion.

Some things originate motion without themselves being in motion, such as objects of desire. The soul, as the form that a living being is oriented toward enacting, is what guides that living being's development; and for the sake of perpetuating this enactment of the form that they are, living things "do whatever they do according to nature" (*On the Soul* II.4, 415b1-2). Soul in this sense is an unmoved mover for all living beings, the natural inner principle in accord with which they are self-moved. Soul moves as an end or *telos*, and this is the cornerstone of Aristotle's "teleological" understanding of nature.

While this natural self-orientation of all living things is a kind of desire built into them, animals have desire in a more emphatic sense, because they have perception, and hence experience pleasure and pain; and they have imagination such that those pleasures and pains are associated with the images of the things that occasion them. The "desires" of animals and plants are rather unproblematically ordered to guide their motions toward the fulfillment and sustaining of their natures; and it is desire that Aristotle settles on as the "part" of soul that accounts for the motion of animals (III.10, 433a31-b1). The ultimate cause of a movement is the thing desired, but this has both an immediate sense (the present object that incites desire) and a more comprehensive sense (the continued being of the animal's own soul).

Humans, on the other hand, do exhibit something like a dualistic character. Aristotle brings this out, here as in Book VII of the *Nicomachean Ethics*, by examining the phenomenon of lack of self-command (*akrasia* or "incontinence"). We desire to do A when we know it is better to do B, and in the end we act on the desire rather than the knowledge (III.9, 433a1-3). This seems like a dualistic opposition between reason and desire. Aristotle, however, argues that this is a misleading interpretation, since "intellect is manifestly not a mover without desire; for wish is desire, and whenever one moves according to reasoning, one moves according to wish as well" (III.10, 433a22-25). The opposition between reason and appetite results from an opposition between our desires for two different ends; this state of affairs "comes about in beings that have perception of time, since intellect bids us resist on account of the consequences, while appetite is on account of the immediate (for the immediate appears pleasant, and simply pleasant, and simply good, on account of not seeing the consequences)" (III.10, 433b6-10).

Humans can, however, choose between A and B; we can reflect on both A and B, comparing them as objects of desire that have different consequences. We can do this because, unlike animals which are limited to "sensory imagination," we have "deliberative imagination," the ability to imagine different courses of action and the results to which they may lead. A and B can hold the same place in two hypothetical exercises of imagination. This is due to our possession of reason: "For the question whether one will do this or that is already a work of reasoning, and it always requires a single measure; for one pursues what is better, so that out of many images it is able to produce a single one" (III.11, 434a7-10). Reason's ability to recognize analogous relations enables us to recognize both A and B as the same kind of thing, namely as goods, and to compare them as such so as to determine which is better and ought to be pursued.

Because humans have reason and deliberative imagination, the ordering of our desires toward our natural fulfillment is not so unproblematic as it is in the animals. A variety of possible goods enter into our deliberations, and we do not always look to the consequences or imagine them adequately. Since we compare goods in terms of what is better and less good, we arrange goods in a hierarchy in our imaginations, and deliberative thought invests the images we bear in our imaginations with different degrees of desirability (III.11, 434a10-11). As we come to understand more fully the comparative weight of competing goods, that hierarchical ordering is subject to revision. What it is that fulfills our nature and enables us to fully enact the capacities of our souls is something we have to discover by rational reflection; and this comprehensive good, the active being-fully-itself of our own souls, necessarily puts all the other goods in our imaginative hierarchy into perspective. Aristotle undertakes such comprehensive rational reflection on the fulfillment of our natures and the ordering of our desires (which is to say on the good life) in the *Nicomachean Ethics*.

In one sense, then, it is the *Nicomachean Ethics* that is really about "freedom of the will" as self-motion. If self-motion means taking our own soul in its thriving condition as the object of desire that moves us, it is Aristotle's ethical inquiry that clarifies what that object of desire is, and what is required for it to become effectively the unmoved mover that moves us and orders the desirability of other goods in our imagination. The freedom that this provides is liberation from falsehood in our thoughts and desires. This is what one might call the classical understanding of freedom, as dramatically depicted in Plato's cave allegory at the beginning of *Republic* Book VII: the ability to recognize, choose and pursue what is truly good.

The contribution of *On the Soul* to this understanding of self-motion consists primarily in clarifying the basic psychic powers that make it possible for humans. In the first place, Aristotle provides an alternative to the mechanical model that would depict perception as an external compulsion exercised on the soul by the motions of elemental bodies. Rather, in his account the perceptible thing is the occasion for enabling the sense to be active as fully itself, or what it is oriented toward being. In the second place, the motions incited in an animal through sensing, imagining and desiring are for the sake of enacting and sustaining the being that it is, so that, whatever the material process by which the motion is incited, the ultimate cause is the soul of the animal itself. Finally, in the case of humans, our deliberative imagination and rationality give us the distinctive ability to bring different goods into comparison and to seek the greater goods in preference to the lesser. We act according to our nature when this deliberative capacity works well and effectively governs our choices (III.11, 434a14-15). Choosing well both guides us to the fulfillment of our distinct nature and is partly constitutive of that fulfillment. In all three respects, there is no contradiction between being moved by the object of sense, imagination or desire and being fundamentally self-moved: the animal is always moved, in the decisive sense, by its own soul when it moves in accord with its nature. Aristotle recognizes a fundamental distinction between natural and compulsory motion (I.3, 406a22; cf. *Physics* IV.8, 215a1-6); a mechanistic view of nature cannot ultimately sustain such a distinction, and, indeed, is typically constructed upon the refusal to recognize such a distinction, understanding all motion in terms of compulsion.

To put this final point differently, a mechanical understanding of nature rests upon the principle of pure necessity. It simply is as it is, a cold world of brute fact; and human "values" that issue from consciousness have only the status of projections onto that gray screen. But if, as Aristotle tells us, every living thing is engaged in the fulfillment of its nature, then that nature constitutes the good for that being, so that goodness is a principle of being. Aristotle emphasizes this point several times in the final two chapters of *On the Soul*, in which he reflects upon the necessary relationships among the many powers of soul he has examined, and especially the various senses. Only the sense of touch is, strictly speaking, necessary for animal life. "The other senses are for the sake of living well, and they necessarily pertain already not just to any animal whatsoever, but to certain kinds" (III.12, 434b24-25). The diversity of animal kinds manifests a variety of ways of achieving and enacting the good that is living in this world, moving through it, and discerning the beings that make it up.

Aristotle's final reflection on this theme of diverse (and, one might say, gratuitous) embodiments of the good concerns communication: An animal "has hearing so that something may be signified to it, and a tongue so that it may signify something to another" (III.13, 435b24-25). Though not limited to human speech, this description certainly puts us in mind of it. By the power of speech, humans have a breadth and depth of discernment of the beings that make up the world that is lacking to other animals. It enables us to raise questions, to extend our reflections to first principles, to pass along the record of such efforts to our contemporaries and to subsequent generations. It makes it possible to engage in and share an inquiry as fundamental and comprehensive as *On the Soul* and the inquiries into nature, human life, and the first principles of being and intelligibility in which it occupies a central place. Such inquiry (as Aristotle suggests in the first two chapters of his *Metaphysics*) may be the highest form of freedom and the truest fulfillment of the distinctively human nature.

On the Soul (*De Anima*)

Book One

I.1

We consider knowledge a noble and honorable thing, and one 402a
kind to be more so than another if it is more precise or concerned
with better and more wondrous things. Because it possesses both
these qualifications, we would have good reason to place inquiry
about the soul in the first ranks. Knowledge of it seems, indeed,
to contribute enormously toward all uncovering of truth, but
especially truth about nature—for soul is in some way a governing
principle of living things. We seek to discern and to understand
both its nature and its distinct being[1], and then also whatever
comes along with it (and of these, some seem to be affections[2]
belonging to the soul itself, others rather to come about in living
things because of soul).

But to reach any trustworthy conviction about soul is one of 10
the most difficult of all tasks in every way. Now, since what we
are seeking here is also sought in many other inquiries—I mean
what the thing in question is and its distinct being—one might
think there is some single approach with regard to all things
whose distinct being we wish to understand (just as, regarding the
attributes[3] peculiar to a thing, there is demonstration), so that this
one approach should be sought. But if there is no single common
approach for discerning what a thing is, the undertaking becomes
more difficult, since it will require discovering what the right way
is for each thing. But even if it were clear that it is demonstration
or division into classes or some other approach, there will still be 20

---

1   See Glossary, "Substantial Being"
2   See Glossary, "Affections"
3   See Glossary, "Incidental"

a great deal of puzzling and casting about for the proper starting-points of the inquiry. For different beginnings belong to different inquiries, for example to the study of numbers and to the study of surfaces.

Perhaps it is necessary first to distinguish what it is and in which genus—I mean whether it is a "this" and a substantial being, or a quality or a quantity or some other of the categories that have been distinguished—and then whether it is among things existing as potential or is rather some kind of being-fully-itself (for the difference is not slight).[4]

402b   One must also consider whether it is divisible into parts or indivisible, as well as whether every soul is alike in form or not—and if not, then whether the difference is in form or in genus.[5] Now, those who speak and inquire about soul seem to reflect only about the human soul. But one must take care not to fail to see whether, as the soul of a living thing, it has a single *logos*[6]; or whether, as the soul of a horse, a dog, a human, or a god, it is different for each, while a living thing as a universal is either nothing at all or something secondary. (We should do the same in any other case where things are called by a common name.) And further, if there are not several souls[7] but rather parts of soul, there

10   is a question whether it is necessary to seek the whole soul or the parts first. But it is also difficult to determine which parts differ from one another by nature, as well as whether it is necessary to investigate first the parts or their works, e.g. intellect or thinking, the perceptive or perception, and likewise for the rest. But if the works should be first, again one might raise the problem whether their correlatives must be sought before them, e.g. the thing perceived by the perceptive, or the thing thought by the intellect.

Now it seems not only to be the case that understanding what a thing is helps us to see the causes of the attributes belonging to distinct beings (just as, in mathematics, knowing what the straight and curved are, or a line and a plane, is useful for considering

---

4   See Glossary, "Categories", "Potency/Potential", and "Being-fully-itself"

5   In raising the question of likeness of form, Aristotle may have in mind (as the subsequent two sentences also suggest) the "one-soul-fits-all" Pythagorean doctrine according to which the souls of humans are reborn in animals and vice-versa, which would only be possible if all soul had one form.

6   See Glossary, "*Logos*"

7   The question here is whether the different activities of soul belong to different souls within the living being or different parts of one soul.

how many right angles the angles of a triangle equal), but also the   20
attributes in turn contribute a great deal toward understanding
what it is. For when we are able to give an account of all or most
of the attributes in accord with our mental image, then we will
also be able to speak most excellently about the distinct being[8],
since every demonstration begins from what something is. So, as
for definitions that do not lead to knowledge of the attributes nor
even the ability to conjecture them easily, it is clear that they are   403a
all given dialectically and vacuously.

There is also perplexity about the affections of the soul: are
they all also shared by the thing that has soul, or is any of them
peculiar to the soul itself? This is necessary to understand, but
not easy. In most of these cases the soul appears not to act or be
affected separately from the body, for example in the cases of
being angered, being emboldened, desiring, and perceiving in
general. Thinking seems most of all peculiar to soul; but if this is
some kind of imagination or does not occur without imagination,
then it would not be able to exist without a body. So then if one of
the works or affections of the soul is peculiar to it, soul could be   10
separate. But if nothing is peculiar to it, it would not be separate—
just like a straight thing, to which, as straight, many attributes
belong, such as to touch a bronze sphere at a point, while "the
straight," if separated, will not touch it this way; for it is not
separable if in fact it is always found together with a body. But all
the affections of the soul seem to be found together with a body
too—spiritedness, gentleness, fear, pity, boldness, and also joy and
loving and hating—for along with these the body is affected in
some way. An indication of this is that at one time powerful and
vivid affections do not provoke or frighten us, but at other times
small and faint ones move us, whenever the body is worked up   20
and in such a condition as it is when it is angered. And this is even
clearer: when nothing frightening is happening we fall into the
state of feeling of one who is frightened.

---

8   For example, owls are distinct beings with certain attributes, like having
     a particular kind of beak. If we want to know why the beak is the way
     it is, it would be useful to have a clear sense of what an owl is (a kind of
     nocturnal bird predatory upon rodents). But also if we could give some
     account of all the proper attributes that fill out an accurate image of the
     owl (its particular kind of eyes, wings, talons, bodily proportions, etc.),
     this might help us to gain a clear sense of what kind of thing the owl is
     (especially if we contrast them with the corresponding attributes of, say,
     a robin).

If this is so, it is clear that the affections occurring in the soul are *logoi* in material. Thus their definitions will be like this: "being angered is a certain motion of such a sort of body or part or potency, caused by this and aiming at that." Hence it is clear that it belongs to the student of nature to give attention to soul, either all soul or soul of this sort. But the student of nature and the dialectician would define each of the affections differently. For example, what is anger? For the latter, it is the desire to reciprocate pain or some such thing; for the former, it is a boiling of blood or something hot around the heart. The one gives an account of the material, the other of the form and the *logos*; but, though this is the *logos* of the thing, it must be in this sort of material if it is going to be at all. In the same way, the *logos* of the house is, let us say, that it is a shelter preventing destruction by winds, rainstorms and scorching heat; but the other will call it stones, bricks and beams. But another may call it the form in these things for the sake of those ends.

Which of these is the student of nature? Is it the one who speaks about the material, ignoring the form, or the one concerned only with the *logos*? Or is it rather the one combining both? But in that case who is each of the others? Or is no one concerned with the affections of material that are neither separable nor treated as separable? The student of nature is concerned with all the works and affections of a certain sort of body and a certain sort of material, while for other sorts it is someone else. Concerning some it may be a craftsman such as a carpenter or doctor, while the mathematician treats of non-separable things as if they were not occurrences in such a body but abstracted from it, and the practitioner of first philosophy treats of separable things.[9]

But (to return to the point from which this last discourse began) we were saying that the affections of the soul are inseparable from the natural material of the living thing, and in particular the material to which these particular kinds of things (like spiritedness and fear) belong—but inseparable in a different way than a line or surface.

I.2

In inquiring about soul, it is necessary not only to examine the perplexities about which we must gain understanding in order to move forward; we must also see what aid is available from the

---

9   See Glossary, "First Philosophy".

opinions of those of our predecessors who had something to say about it, so that we may take up what has been well said and be on guard against anything not well said. The starting point for such an inquiry is a setting forth of the things thought most of all to belong by nature to soul. The ensouled is thought to differ from the soulless above all in two things: in motion and in perception. And it is pretty much these two thoughts that we have inherited from our forebears concerning soul.

For many of them say that soul is primarily and above all a mover. And since they thought something that was not in motion could not move something else, they took soul to be among things that are in motion. Hence Democritus[10] says it is some kind of fire or heat; for, atoms or shapes being limitless, he calls the spherical ones fire and soul (comparable to the so-called motes in the air, which are seen in sunbeams that come in through windows). He calls these seeds collectively the elements of the whole of nature (and Leucippus[11] does likewise); and the spherical ones among them he calls soul since these, by having such shape, are most able to slip into other things and move them, being in motion themselves. For these men understand soul to be what gives animals their motion.

Hence they understand respiration to be coextensive with living. For when the surrounding atmosphere masses against bodies and drives out the atomic shapes that give the animals their motion (by being never at rest themselves), reinforcements come from outside when similar ones rush in to replace them during respiration. Since these also prevent the ones remaining in the animals from being expelled, fortifying them against the pressing forces and regrouping them, the animals continue to live as long as they are able to do this.

What is said by the Pythagoreans[12] seems to contain the same thought too, for some of them said that soul is the motes in the air, others that it is what moves these. This is because, as has been said, they seem to be always in motion, even in a completely windless calm.

30

404a

10

---

10   Democritus of Abdera (born c.460 BC) explained natural beings in terms of tiny particles ("atoms", or "indivisibles").

11   Teacher of Democritus, and probably the first to develop the doctrine of atomism.

12   A school of thinkers explaining all things in terms of mathematics (especially numbers), they claimed to follow Pythagoras of Samos (6th cent. BC), though it is unclear how central mathematics was to the thought of Pythagoras himself.

20   And those who say the soul is what moves itself are borne along to the same point.[13] They all seem to have understood motion to be the thing most characteristic of soul and all other things to be in motion because of soul, while it is moved by itself (for they saw nothing imparting motion that was not itself in motion).

Anaxagoras[14] similarly says that soul is what imparts motion, as does anyone else who has said that mind[15] set the whole of things in motion. (This is not at all what Democritus says, who simply identifies soul and mind; for he equates what is true with

30   what appears, and so approves of Homer's verse in which Hector "lay stricken, and altered in mind."[16] He does not use "mind" to mean a certain potency concerned with truth, but uses "soul"

404b   and "mind" interchangeably.) But Anaxagoras speaks less clearly about these things. In some cases he says that the cause of what is beautifully and properly done is mind, in other cases that it is soul (for he says it belongs to all animals, the great and the small, the honorable and the contemptible). But mind, or at any rate what is called thoughtful mind, does not appear to belong in a similar way to all animals—nor indeed to all human beings.

Those, then, who focused on the being in motion of what is ensouled understood soul to be that which most of all imparts motion. But those who focused on its recognition and perception

10   of beings say that soul is the primordial principles of things, whether they made these out to be many or one. Thus according to Empedocles, soul is composed of all the elements, but is also each one of these. He says:

> For it is by means of earth that earth comes to sight,
> Water by water, by ether the ether bright,
> By fire, fire that brings to all things their perdition,
> By Love, Love, Contention by baneful Contention.[17]

---

13   Plato characterizes the soul this way in *Phaedrus* 245b-e and *Laws* 895b.

14   Anaxagoras of Clazomenae (c.500-428 BC) taught that the elements that constitute natural beings were put into order by Mind (*nous*). He was also an advisor to the Athenian statesman Pericles.

15   I have translated the Greek word *nous* as "mind" when referring broadly to what we would call "consciousness" (as Aristotle's predecessors tend to use it) and as "intellect" when Aristotle means to speak of it in distinction from other cognitive potencies. (See Glossary, "Intellect.")

16   This line occurs at *Iliad* 23.698, but Hector is not the subject there.

17   According to Aristotle, Empedocles of Agrigentum (c.492-432 BC) treated the first four (earth, water, air and fire) as material constitutives of all things and the last two (love and contention or strife) as the principles of attraction and repulsion between them (*Metaphysics* 988a27ff.).

In the same way Plato too, in the *Timaeus*, makes the soul be composed out of the elements; it is posited that like is known by like and that things are composed from the primordial principles. Likewise in the discourses on philosophy[18] the view is delineated that "living being itself" is composed of the idea of the One and   20
of the primordial length, breadth and depth, as all other things are in a similar way. And it is also said, starting from another direction, that intellect is the One, deductive knowledge the Two (since it proceeds in a single direction to one result), opinion the number of the plane and perception the number of the solid.[19] So then, on the one hand, the numbers are said to be the forms and primordial principles, but are composed of elements; while on the other hand things are distinguished either by intellect or by knowledge, opinion or perception, and the forms of the things are the corresponding numbers. And since, in addition to being able to thus cognize, the soul seemed able to impart motion, some people tangled it up from both threads and declared soul to be a number that moves itself.

These predecessors differ over the primordial principles,   30
both over what they are and over how many—especially those who make them corporeal and those who make them incorporeal, and further those who mix these and declare that the primordial   405a
principles derive from both kinds of elements. As for those who differ concerning the number, some say there is one and others more than one. And they interpret soul in ways that follow these doctrines, since, not unreasonably, they take it to be whatever among the primary things is of such a nature as to impart motion.

Hence it seemed to some of them to be fire, since this is the most subtly composed and least corporeal of the elements, and is moreover in motion and preeminent for setting other things in motion. Democritus has most elegantly explained why these are both so: soul (which for him is the same as mind) is one of the   10
primary and indivisible bodies, productive of motion because of the smallness and shape of its particles; he says the spherical is the most mobile of figures, and that mind and fire are of such shape.

Anaxagoras however, as we said above, seems sometimes to say that mind and soul are different, and at other times treats both

---

18   An unknown text.

19   "The number of the plane" is 3 (since three points are required to define a plane surface) and "the number of the solid" is 4.

as one nature, except that he posits mind as the most primordial principle of all (at any rate, he says it is the only being that is simple, unmixed and pure). But he explains both cognizing and moving by means of the same governing principle, saying that mind set the whole of things in motion.

20   Thales[20] too, on the report of those who preserve recollections of him, seems to have taken soul to be something imparting motion, if he did in fact say that the magnet has a soul because it moves iron.

Diogenes[21], like some others, took it to be air, considering this to be the most subtly composed of all things and to be the primordial principle. This, he said, is why soul cognizes and moves things, cognizing insofar as it is primary and the rest are composed of it, and able to impart motion inasmuch as it is subtlest.

Heraclitus[22] also says that soul is the primordial principle since, according to him, it is vapor, out of which he constructs the rest. It is most incorporeal and ever flowing, and what is in motion is cognized by what is in motion. He (and most of the others) considered beings to be in motion.

And Alcmaeon[23] seems to have had pretty much the same
30   notions about soul as these others. He says it is immortal due to its likeness to the immortals. This belongs to it by virtue of its being always in motion, since all divine things (the moon, the sun, the stars and the whole heavens) are always in continuous motion.

405b   Among the cruder thinkers, some have even declared that it is water, such as Hippo[24]. (They seem to have been persuaded of this on the basis of the generative seed of all things being wet.) For he refuted those who said blood is soul by saying that generative

---

20   Thales of Miletus (7th-6th cent. BC) is one of the ancient "Seven Sages" and often considered the first Greek philosopher.

21   Diogenes of Apollonia (5th cent. BC) followed Anaximenes of Miletus (6th cent. BC) in teaching that all things are composed of condensed or dilated air. As Aristotle suggests, Diogenes seems to have reinterpreted the thought of Anaxagoras by identifying Mind (which Anaxagoras at times suggests is immaterial) with the material element air.

22   Heraclitus of Ephesus (6th-5th cent. BC) was famous for emphasizing the difficulty of pinning down the identity of anything in a constantly changing world.

23   Alcmaeon of Croton (5th century BC) is an obscure (possibly Pythagorean) figure, mentioned here and in *Metaphysics* I.5.

24   Hippo, an obscure thinker (5th century BC), is treated even more dismissively in *Metaphysics* I.3.

seed is not blood, and that it is the first soul. But others, such as Critias[25], said that it is blood. They took perception to be most characteristic of soul and to belong to things by virtue of the nature of blood.

Each of the elements has found someone to award it the prize except for earth; no one has spoken up for it, except if someone has said that soul is composed of all the elements or is all of them.   10

So one may say, then, that everyone distinguishes the soul by three things: motion, perception and incorporeality. And each of these gets traced back to the primordial principles. Thus those who distinguish it by cognition make it be an element or composed of elements, speaking pretty similarly to one another (with one exception). For they say that like is recognized by like; and since soul cognizes all things, they construct it out of all the primordial principles. As many as say there is one cause and one element posit also the soul as one, such as fire or air. But most, saying that the primordial principles are multiple, make the soul multiple too. Only Anaxagoras says that mind is unaffected and   20 has nothing in common with any other thing. But if it is such, how and by what cause will it come to know? This he has not said, nor is it quite clear from the things he has said.

Those who make there be oppositions among the primordial principles also construct the soul out of opposites. But those who opt for one of the opposites, such as heat or cold or some other such thing, also similarly posit the soul to be some one of them. Thus they sometimes also follow the trail of names, some saying it is heat because living is named after it, others that it is cold, because breathing and cooling are called "soul." [26]

These, then, are what have been handed down to us concerning soul and the reasons for saying them.   30

I.3

First, what concerns motion must be examined. For not only may it be the case that its distinct being is not such as those people   406a

---

25   Critias (c.460-403 BC), a significant Athenian political figure and cousin of Plato, appears in several Platonic dialogues. He had a reputation for impiety and atheism, and was one of the "Thirty Tyrants" who ruled Athens after its defeat in the Peloponnesian War.

26   The first etymology derives "zen" (to live) from "zein" (to boil); the second observes the similarities among the words for soul (psyche), cold (psychron) and cooling (katapsyxis). "Psyche" originally means "breath," and breathing was thought to help keep the body cool.

assert who say that soul is what moves itself or is able to impart motion, but it might even be an impossibility for motion to belong to it.

That it is not indeed necessary for what imparts motion to be itself in motion has been said already.[27]

There are two ways in which anything is moved: in virtue of something else or in virtue of itself. We say things are moved in virtue of something else if they are in something that is in motion, like sailors. For the way they are moved is not like the way the boat is moved, since it is moved in virtue of itself while they are moved by being in something that is in motion. This is clear if we look to their parts: for walking is the characteristic motion of feet and so also of human beings, but it does not belong to sailors

10 when sailing. So, there being two ways in which a thing is said to be moved, we are now examining whether soul is moved and partakes in motion in virtue of itself.

Now, since there are four kinds of motion (locomotion, alteration, diminution and growth), it would be moved in one or several or all of these ways. And if it is moved non-incidentally, motion would belong to it by nature, and so also would being in a place, since all the aforesaid motions are in a place. And if *moving itself* is the soul's distinct being, its being moved will not belong to it incidentally, as it does to what is white or what is three feet long.

20 These things are moved, but only incidentally, since that to which they belong, a body, is what is moved; hence, too, they are not in a place. But the soul will be in a place if it does indeed partake in motion by nature.

Moreover, if it is in motion by nature, it could also be moved by force; and if by force, also by nature. The same holds too with respect to rest: where a thing is moved by nature, it rests by nature, and similarly where it is moved by force it rests by force. What sorts of forced motions and rests of the soul there will be is not easy to explain, not even for those who are willing to craft fictions.

Furthermore, if it moves up, it will be fire, and if it moves down, earth, for those are the motions of these bodies; and the same *logos* pertains to the intermediate elements.

30 And further, since it manifestly moves the body, it is reasonable that soul imparts to the body the same motions as those by which it is moved. But if so, then those asserting the converse will also speak the truth, that it is moved by the same motion as that by

---

27   403b28-31; cf. *Physics* VIII.5

which the body is moved. But the body is moved in locomotion,   406b
so that the soul too would change with respect to place, relocating
either as a whole or in part. But if this were possible, then it would
also be possible for it to reenter once it has left; and from this it
would follow that living things that have died could revive.

With respect to incidental motion, it could be moved by
something else, since an animal may be shoved by force. But, if
being self-moved is in something's distinct being, it ought not
to be moved by something else, unless incidentally (just as what
is good through itself or by virtue of itself ought not to be good   10
through something else or for the sake of something else). One
might, though, most plausibly say that the soul is moved by the
things it perceives, if it is indeed moved.

But to be sure, even if the soul just moves itself, still it would
be moved. So, if every motion is a departure of the thing moved
in the respect in which it is moved, the soul would depart from its
distinct being if, rather than moving itself incidentally, the motion
is of its distinct being itself with respect to itself.[28]

Some also say that the way the soul moves the body it is in
is the same way it is itself moved, such as Democritus. He speaks
more or less like Phillipus the comic poet, who has Daedalus make
a wooden Aphrodite that moves by pouring quicksilver into her.
Democritus speaks similarly because he claims that the atomic   20
spheres, being of such a nature as to never stay put, drag the whole
body along with them and impart motion to it. We, however,
shall ask whether this same thing produces rest; and it is difficult,
indeed impossible, to say how it will. More generally, the soul does
not seem to move the animal this way, but rather through some
kind of choice and thinking.

In the same way, Timaeus gives a natural explanation
according to which the soul moves the body, saying that by
moving itself it also moves the body because of its entwinement
with it. Once the soul had been constituted from the elements
and divided up according to harmonic numbers, so that it might   30
have an innate perception of harmony and that the whole might
move in harmonious motions, he bent its straight path around

---

28   In other words, it is incoherent to identify self-motion as the very being of
something. If soul is identified with self-motion, then what will it mean
for it to move *itself*? If self-motion is changed, it becomes something
other than self-motion. This result is, in a way, the absurd opposite of
what Aristotle will argue: that the soul is what is responsible for a living
thing's maintaining itself as what it is.

into a circle. And, after dividing this one circle into two that touch each other in two places, he divided one of them again into seven circles—as though the revolutions of the heavens were also the motions of the soul.[29]

407a

Now, in the first place, it is just not right to say that the soul is a magnitude; for, as for the soul of the whole, it is clear that he intends it to be something of such a sort as what is called intellect. (It certainly cannot be such a sort as perceptive soul, nor as desiring soul, since the motion of these is not circular.) Intellect, however, is one and continuous in just the way thought is. But thought is the things thought, and these are one by way of their succession, as number is and not as magnitude is;[30] hence neither is intellect continuous in this way, but is either without parts or at any rate not continuous in the way any magnitude is.

10

And really, how will it even think if it is a magnitude? By means of some one of its own parts? Parts in the sense of magnitude or in the sense of a point (if one ought to speak of these too as parts)? Now, if it is in the sense of a point, since these are infinite it is clear that it will never make it through to the end.[31] But if it is in the sense of a magnitude, it will often, or rather infinitely often, think the same thing; but it is manifestly capable of thinking something

---

29 Aristotle here summarizes parts of Plato's *Timaeus* (primarily 35b-37a), which he spends the rest of chapter 3 undermining with objections. The speaker, Timaeus of Locri, tells a "likely story" about the origins of the cosmos. Aristotle gives a précis of a passage in which Timaeus describes the fashioning of the "world-soul," or the form that governs the motion of the cosmos, which serves as a model for all souls. The first two circles are (1) the path of the cosmos as a whole, which circles the earth's equator, and (2) the path of the sun, which moves obliquely from tropic to tropic. The latter is divided into the paths of the sun and the six known planets. The cosmos is conceived (in accord with what later came to be known as Ptolemaic astronomy) as a starry sphere with the earth at the center, and planets revolving around the earth in motions compounded of their own orbits and the orbit of the outer sphere.

30 In Greek mathematics, numbers are understood as "multitudes of units" (or what we call "natural numbers"), so that they are discrete items in succession, not continuous like magnitudes. Not until Dedekind's treatment of the "number line" are multitudes and magnitudes fully assimilated, though this equivalence is prepared by Descartes' analytic geometry. In parallel to this modern understanding of number, we speak of the "stream of consciousness," whereas for Aristotle our thinking is composed of distinct thoughts about distinct things. What unifies it is its power to take on the forms of intelligible things in succession (See III. 4 and Glossary, "Intellect").

31 Cf. *Physics*, III.6 on the infinite.

just once. And if it is sufficient that it make contact[32] by means of some one of its parts, what need is there for it to move in a circle, or indeed to have magnitude at all? But if it is necessary for it to think by contacting something with its whole circle, what will contact by its parts be? And furthermore, how will it think what has parts by means of what does not, or what does not by means of what does?

This circle must of necessity be the intellect. For thinking   20
is the motion of intellect, while revolving is that of a circle; if, then, thinking is revolving, then intellect would be the circle whose revolving in this way is thinking. So what thing will it be always thinking (as it must if its revolving is unending)? In all cases of practical thinking there are end-points, since they are all for the sake of something, while contemplative thinking is similarly bounded by *logoi*. But every *logos* is either a definition or a demonstration. Now, demonstrations proceed from a starting point and in some way reach an end, either a deduction or a conclusion; and even if they do not conclude, still they do not at all turn back again toward their starting point, but rather proceed in a straight line, always adding another mean or extreme. A   30
revolving motion, however, turns back again to its starting point. (Definitions, for their part, are all limited.) And if, moreover, it goes through the same revolving motion many times, it will have to think the same thing many times.

Moreover, thinking seems more like stillness and coming to rest than like a motion (and the same goes for a deduction). And surely, nothing can be blissful that is forced rather than easy; but   407b
if self-motion is not its distinct being, then it would be moved contrary to nature.[33] (It would also be burdensome to be mingled with the body and unable to get free from it; indeed, it would be something to be avoided, if it is in fact better for the soul not to be with the body, which is commonly said and also seems to many to be the case.[34]) But it is also unclear what the cause is of the heaven's

---

32   Timaeus (37a) speaks of the soul's knowing things in terms of its contact with them. He also makes the distinction between its contacting things with and without parts, though it is not clear what he makes of that distinction.

33   According to Timaeus the soul is set into motion after it has been formed, and so is not identified with self-motion though it is characterized by self-motion; cf. *Timaeus* 34b, 36e and 37b, and 406b12-15 above.

34   An argument for this opinion is put forward by Socrates in Plato's *Phaedo*, esp. 64e-67c. Thus it could be said to be a Platonic doctrine, with which the account of the cosmic soul in the *Timaeus* conflicts.

being moved in a circle. For the soul's distinct being is not the cause of motion in a circle, but it is moved this way incidentally (and even less is the body the cause than the soul). Nor, indeed, is it said that it is so because it is better to be so. Yet it surely ought
10   to have been because of this that the god made the soul be moved in a circle, namely because it is better for it to be in motion than to stand still, and to be moved this way rather than another.[35] But, since such an inquiry is more appropriate for other discourses, let us set it aside for now.

There is something odd, though, incident to this discourse [of Timaeus] as well as to most that are concerned with soul: they put the soul into a body and join them together without further determining the cause of this or what the body is fit for. Yet this would seem to be necessary, since through their association one acts and the other is acted upon, one is moved and the other moves it; reciprocal relations such as these do not belong to just
20   any chance things. Some undertake only to say what sort of thing the soul is, but concerning the body that receives it they make no further determination, as if they accept, as the Pythagorean stories have it, that any chance soul gets clothed in any chance body. But on the contrary, each seems to have its peculiar form and shape. They speak pretty nearly as someone would who said that carpentry is embodied in flutes; for each art must use its own tools, and each soul its own body.

I.4

There is, in addition, a certain other opinion about soul that has been passed along, which, to many, is not any less persuasive than the ones discussed. It has presented its arguments—public depositions, as it were—in discourses that have gone into wider
30   circulation.[36] For they say that soul is a certain harmony, since they also say that harmony is a blending and agreement of opposites and that the body is composed of opposites. A harmony, however, is a certain ratio [logos] or agreement of the things mixed, whereas the soul cannot be either of these things. Furthermore, imparting
408a   motion is not characteristic of harmony, but this is what everyone, so to speak, allots most of all to soul.

---

35   This basic premise is enunciated earlier in Timaeus' account (cf.29e), but, as Aristotle observes, is not invoked in the discussion of the cosmic motion.

36   Aristotle may refer to writings such as Plato's *Phaedo* (cf. 85e-88d, 92a-95a, which suggests that the idea may be Pythagorean in origin).

It is more in tune to speak of harmony with respect to health, and to excellences of the body more generally, than with respect to soul. This will be quite evident if one should try to give an explanation of the affections and works of the soul by means of some harmony, for it will be difficult to bring into tune.

Moreover, if we speak of harmony, we have two things in sight. Above all, it is the agreement of the magnitudes in things that have position and motion, whenever they are so fitted with one another as to allow nothing that is the same in kind to enter in; and derivatively, we speak of the ratio of the things mixed.[37] Neither way makes sense with respect to soul. As to the agreement between parts of the body, it is easy to discover the flaw. For the parts have multiple and multifarious agreements; of what, then, or in what way, must one understand the intellect or the perceiving or desiring part to be an agreement? Similarly, it is also strange for the soul to be the ratio of the mixture, for the mixture of the elements in virtue of which something is flesh does not have the same ratio as that in virtue of which it is bone. It will turn out, then, that one has many souls and has them all over the whole body, if all the parts are composed of mixtures of elements and the ratio of the mixture is a harmony and a soul. (One might demand that Empedocles explain at least this much. For he says that each of the parts is what it is in virtue of some ratio. Is it, then, that the soul is the ratio, or is it rather something else that comes to be in the parts? Furthermore, is Friendship the cause of whatever mixture there chances to be or of a mixture according to a ratio, and is it itself the ratio or something else aside from the ratio?)[38]

10

20

---

37   "Harmony" applies above all to what we would call the commensurability of wavelengths produced by two sounding bodies. Aristotle, on the basis of Pythagorean studies of musical harmonies, understood this commensurability in terms of the lengths of strings: two strings of the same thickness will produce harmonies if their lengths are in the ratio of small whole numbers, such as 1:2 or 2:3 (ratios such that no other number or length stuck in between will maintain the harmony). The ratios of the numbers, in turn, are also called harmonic. Pythagoreans, however, would reverse the direction of dependence, saying that the numbers are more real than the things whose behavior they determine. Aristotle argues against them that numbers are only abstractions of the mind (cf. *Metaphysics* XIV.3, 1090a31–b2). It is important to recall that the Greeks considered one to be a unit, and numbers to be multitudes of units; for Aristotle the principle of unity of a thing is a deep aspect of the reality of that thing–and soul is such a principle–but the numbers that tell us how many unities happen to be present have a derivative kind of reality.

38   For the role of Friendship in Empedocles, see note to 404b15.

Such are the perplexities involved in these ideas. If, on the other hand, the soul is something different from the mixture, what, then, may be the reason that it is lost at the same time that what makes the flesh be flesh is lost (and the same for the other parts of the animal)? And if, in addition to this, it is not the case that the soul is the ratio of the mixture and that each of the parts has a soul, what is it that is lost when the soul leaves?

30   So then, that the soul can neither be a harmony nor revolve in a circle is clear from what has been said.

It is, though, possible, as we have said, for it to be moved incidentally, and also to move itself; such is the case when that in which it resides is moved, and is moved by the soul. In no other way can the soul be moved with respect to place.

But one might reasonably be perplexed about the soul as

408b   something that is moved, if one considers the following. We speak of the soul as being pained and rejoicing, or being bold and frightened, as well as getting angry and perceiving and being thoughtful, and all these seem to be motions; hence one might believe that it is moved. But this is not necessarily so. For, even if it is as true as can be that to be pained or to rejoice or to be thoughtful are motions; and that each of them is a being-moved; and that it is by the soul that their motion is imparted (for example, being angry or being afraid is a particular motion of the heart, and being thoughtful is either the same kind of thing or, perhaps, something

10   else); and that some of these turn out to be changes in place of the things moved and others alterations (but how and of what sort is another discussion)—nonetheless, to say that the soul is angry is as if someone were to say the soul is weaving or building. It is perhaps better to say, not that the soul pities or learns or thinks, but that the human being does these due to the soul. But this is not a case of the motion being in the soul, but rather it sometimes terminates at the soul and at other times proceeds from it (e.g. perception originates from things present, whereas recollection, proceeding from the soul, results in either motions in the organs of sense or in persisting states of them).

Intellect, however, seems to come about in us as some substantial being, and not to be destroyed. For, though it would be

20   destroyed most of all by the dying of the light that comes with old age, in fact it is in the same case as the organs of sense: if an old man could get hold of an eye like this one, he would see just like a youth. Thus old age consists in something that has happened not to the soul, but to that in which the soul is, just as in inebriations

and diseases. And indeed, thinking and contemplation fades away when something else within is destroyed, while it is in itself imperturbable; but being thoughtful and loving or hating are conditions not of this, but of what possesses this, and in the way it possesses this. Thus when the latter is destroyed, one neither remembers nor loves, for these did not belong to that other thing, but to the combination, which has perished.[39] But perhaps intellect is something more divine and is imperturbable.

From these things it is clear that the soul is not such a thing   30
as to be moved; and if it is not moved in general, obviously it will not be moved by itself either. So then to say that the soul is a number that moves itself is much more unreasonable than the other things said.[40] Those who say this are stuck not only with the impossibilities already accompanying the thesis that it is moved, but also with those peculiar to saying it is a number.

How is one to understand a unit as something moved—   409a
by what and in what way moved, if it is without parts or differentiation? If it is such as to impart or receive motion, it must be differentiated.[41] Furthermore, since they say that a line when set in motion generates a plane, and a point generates a line, then the motions of the units will be lines as well (since a point is a unit that has position, and it follows immediately from the number being soul that it is somewhere and has a position). Also, if from a number someone subtracts a number or a unit, what is left is a different number; but plants and many animals continue to live when divided, and seem to go on having the same kind of soul.   10

Moreover, there would seem to be no difference between calling them units or tiny little bodies. If the little spheres of Democritus were turned into points, so that what remained was only their multitude, part of the multitude will be imparting motion and part being moved, just as in a continuous magnitude;

---

39   In this passage I have deliberately reproduced the obscurity of Aristotle's pronoun references. He is formulating the thought that memory and love, central elements of individual personality, belong not to intellect as such, but to the combination of intellect and living body that is an individual living human being, and that when this combination no longer persists, neither do memory and love, nor therefore individual personality. He may be reluctant to put forward a clear denial of so sensitive a thesis as personal immortality this early in the discourse, when he has not yet set forth the foundations necessary for such an argument. This he does in III.3-5.

40   This formulation is attributed to Xenocrates of Chalcedon (died c. 314 BC), the third head of the Academy (after Plato and Speusippus).

41   Cf. *Physics* 240b8-9: "That which is without parts cannot be in motion."

for the things we have said are not consequences of any difference in largeness or smallness, but of its being a multitude. Hence it is necessary that there be something to set the units in motion. So then, if in the animal whatever imparts motion is soul, this will be the case in the number as well, so that soul will not be both what imparts motion and what receives it, but only what imparts it. But then how is it possible for this soul to be a unit? It must have **20** something that differentiates it from the other units, but what would differentiate a point-unit other than its position?[42]

Now, if the units in the body are not the same thing as the points, the units will be in the same place, for they will each occupy the territory of a point; but then what, indeed, prevents an infinite number from being in the same place, if two are? For the things whose place is indivisible are themselves indivisible. On the other hand, if the points in the body are the number of the soul (or if the number of points in the body is the soul), why don't all bodies have soul, since there seem to be points in all of them, and an infinite number too?

Furthermore, how will the points be able to be separated and **30** released from their bodies, if it is the case that lines do not divide into points?[43]

I.5

Just as we said, then, this turns out, in a way, to say the same thing as those who make the soul out to be some fine-grained body. In another way, it has a peculiar difficulty just like that of **409b** Democritus' account of the body being moved by the soul: If the soul is present in the whole of the perceiving body, and if soul is a body, then it is necessary for two bodies to be in the same place; while for those who say it is a number, there will be many points at one point, or every body will have a soul (unless some

---

42 This argument works simultaneously against Democritus and Xenocrates. If the point-units are sometimes imparting motion and sometimes receiving, and if it is the ones imparting motion that are to be taken as soul, these will be constantly changing from soul to not-soul and back (hence Democritus is wrong to simply identify them as soul), so that the number of them that count as soul will always be changing (hence no particular number will correlate to soul and it will have no unity).

43 A line does not divide into points because it is infinitely divisible in potential, whereas the point is a place where the line is in fact divided or terminated. There is no point present before it is identified as such, and it is always possible to posit more of them within any stretch of the line.

other number turns up that is different from the number of points present in the body). The animal turns out to be moved by the number just the way we said Democritus makes it be moved—for what is the difference between speaking of small spheres and large units (or in general of units being in motion), since either way the motion in which they are moved must necessarily be the one that moves the animal? 10

So those who have tangled up motion and number into one thing end up with these implications and many others like them; for it is impossible not only to define the soul in such a way, but also to account thus for its attributes. This would be evident if one were to try to explain on the basis of this account the acts and affections of the soul, like calculations, perceptions, pleasures, pains or any other such things. As we said at first, it would not be easy to get any intimation of them starting from these oracular pronouncements.

Again, our predecessors have passed on to us three ways by which they demarcate the soul. Some have called it the ultimate 20 mover since it moves itself, while others have called it the most finely-grained body or the most incorporeal of all; we have pretty well gone through the perplexities and contradictions these involve. It remains to examine the way it is said to be composed of the elements. They say this so that it may be able to perceive the things that are and to recognize each of them; but many impossibilities necessarily follow for this account.

They posit that like recognizes like, as if they were positing that the things recognized are the soul. But there exist not only these elements, but many other things besides—or perhaps it is better to say that the things composed of them are unlimited in number. Well then, let us grant that the soul recognizes and perceives the 30 things each of these is made of; still, by what means will it come to know or perceive the whole made of them (for example what a god or a human is, or what flesh or bone is)? Likewise with any other 410a composite: it is not by having the elements combined any old way whatever, but by means of some ratio [*logos*] and composition that each is what it is. Empedocles says this very thing about bone:

> When bountiful Earth in her cauldrons wide
> Had two of eight parts from the bright salt Sea
> And four from Hephaistos, white bone came to be.

It is no use, then, for the elements to be in the soul if the composition and the ratios are not there as well; each thing will

come to know what is like it, but not bone or man, unless these
10 are in the soul too. It hardly needs saying that this is impossible.
Would anyone wonder whether there is a stone or a human being
in the soul? Or likewise the Good or Not-good? And the same goes
for all the other things.

In addition, since being is meant in many ways (for at one time
it indicates a "this something", at another a quantity or a quality
or some other of the categories that have been distinguished), will
the soul be composed of all these or not? There do not, however,
seem to be elements shared by all of these. Will soul then be
composed only of those that are substantial beings? How then
will it know each of the other kinds of being? Or will they say
that there are elements and primordial principles proper to each
20 genus of being, and that soul is composed of them? Then it will
be a quantity and a quality as well as a substantial being. But it is
impossible for something composed of the elements of quantity
to be a substantial being rather than a quantity. These things and
others like them follow for those who say they are composed of
all of them.

It is strange as well to say both that like is unaffected by like
and that like is perceived by like or like is recognized by like, since
they posit that perceiving (and also thinking and recognizing) is
being affected and being moved.

What has just been said serves as testimony to the many
perplexities and difficulties involved in saying, as Empedocles
does, that each thing is recognized by means of bodily elements
30 and in relation to its like. For whatever parts in the bodies of
410b animals are made merely of earth, such as bones and tendons and
hair, seem not to perceive at all; so neither do they perceive their
likes, though this was supposed to be proper to them.

Besides this, more cases of ignorance than of comprehension
will befall each of the primordial principles, since each will
recognize one thing but be ignorant of many (i.e. all those that
differ from it). For Empedocles, indeed, it will turn out that the
god is the stupidest of all, because he alone will not have any
acquaintance with one of the elements, Strife, while all mortal
things will (since each one is composed of all of them).

And in general, why don't all beings have a soul if every one of
them is either an element or composed of one or more elements or
all of them? For in that case each necessarily recognizes one thing
10 or some or all things.

One might also be at a loss concerning what it may be that gives things their unity. The elements, at least, seem more like material, whereas that which holds a thing together, whatever it may be, is the most decisive factor. It is impossible that there be something superior ruling the soul, and this is even more impossible in relation to the intellect. It is in accord with reason that the latter be by nature the most original and decisive thing, whereas *they* say that the elements are primary among the beings.

All those who say that the soul, because it recognizes and perceives beings, is composed of the elements, as well as those who say it is the most productive of movement, fail to speak about every soul. It is not the case that all perceiving things are mobile. There appear to be some animals that are stationary, even though supposedly motion in place is the only motion the soul imparts to an animal. Those who make the elements responsible for intellect and the perceptive power likewise fall short, since plants seem to be alive but to have no share in motion or perception, and many animals are incapable of thinking. Now even if one were to give way on these points and to posit that intellect is some part of the soul (and likewise for the perceptive power), he would still not yet be speaking about every soul, or even about the whole of any soul. (The account in the so-called Orphic poems suffers from this defect as well, for it says that the soul, borne upon the winds, is drawn into things from the whole universe when they breathe; but this can't happen in plants and several kinds of animals, if it is indeed the case that not all things breathe—a point overlooked by those who have accepted such a concept.)

Anyway, if one must make the soul be composed of the elements, one need not compose it from all of them. One term of each pair of opposites is sufficient for judging both itself and its opposite: the straight serves us for judging both itself and the curved, for a straight edge is the measure of both (but the curved is a measure neither of itself nor of the straight).

Now some also say that soul is mingled in the whole of things; hence it is, perhaps, that Thales thought all things were full of gods. But this involves some perplexities. Why is it that the soul, when it is in air or fire, does not make it a living thing, but does so in mixtures—especially if, as it seems to them, it exists more perfectly in the former states? [44] (One might also wish to ask why

20

30
411a

10

---

44   Aristotle seems here to refer to those who identify soul with one of the
     elements because of its mobility, and who thus imply that it is more itself
     in its unmixed and more mobile state.

the soul in the air is more perfect and immortal than when in animals.) Either way, something strange and unreasonable follows. For, to be sure, saying that fire or air is living is among the most unreasonable of things; and not to call something living when there is soul in it is strange. Their conception of the soul as being in these elements seems to rest on the homogeneity of the whole with its parts; hence it is necessary for them to say as well that soul is homogeneous with its parts, if it is by something being drawn from the surrounding atmosphere into these animals that the animals become ensouled. But if the inhaled air is homogeneous and the soul is non-homogeneous, it is clear that something will exist in the latter that does not belong to the former. Thus it is necessary either that the soul be homogeneous or that it not be indiscriminately present in the whole of things.

20

From what has been said, then, it is clear, first, that the presence of recognition in the soul is not due to its being composed of elements, and, second, that it is not well nor truly said that it is in motion. Since, however, recognizing belongs to soul, as do both perceiving and opining, and also appetite and wishing and the desires in general, and motion with respect to place originates in animals from the soul, as do growth and maturation and decline, is it the case that each of these belongs to the soul as a whole, and that it is with all of it that we think and perceive and move and do or undergo each of the other things, or do different things belong to different parts of it? And what about living? Is it in some one of these or in more than one or all of them, or is something else responsible for it? Some, of course, say that the soul has parts, and that it thinks by way of one and has appetite by way of another. But what then holds the soul together, if by nature it is in parts? Certainly not the body, since it seems rather that, on the contrary, the soul holds the body together; at least, when the soul has left it, it dissolves and rots. So if there is some other thing that makes the soul be one, that thing would more properly be soul. But then it will be necessary to inquire again whether that thing is one or has multiple parts. And if it is one, then why could the soul not already have been one? But if it has parts, then the argument will again ask for the thing that holds this together, and of course will go on this way indefinitely.

30
411b

10

Then again, concerning its parts, one might be perplexed about what potency each one has in the body. For if the whole soul holds all the body together, it is fitting that each of its parts hold together some part of the body. But this seems like an impossibility:

it is hard even to imagine what sort of part the intellect will hold together, and in what way. Also, plants clearly continue to live when they are cut in two, and even among animals some of the insects do, as if they go on having souls that are the same in kind, even if not in number: each of the parts has perception and moves with respect to place for awhile. But if the parts don't live on, that isn't at all strange, since they don't have the organs needed to preserve their nature. Nevertheless, in each of the parts all the parts of the soul are present; and these souls are of the same kind as one another and as the former whole, as though on the one hand the "parts" of the soul are inseparable from one another, while on the other hand the soul as a whole is divisible.

20

The governing principle in plants[45] seems indeed to be some kind of soul, since this alone is shared by both plants and animals; and while it does exist separately from the perceptive principle, nothing has perception without this.

---

45   That is, the governing principle responsible for growth, maturation and decay.

Book Two

II.1

412a3   As for what has been handed down by our predecessors concerning soul, let that suffice. For our part, let us come at it again as if from the beginning, attempting to delineate what soul is and what would be the *logos* most common to all soul.

Among beings we acknowledge a certain kind called substantial being. One way of being substantial is as material, which is not by itself a distinct something; another way is shape and form, by which it is immediately distinguished as something; a third way is as a composite of these two. The material is potential;

10   the form is being-fully-itself, in two ways: either as knowledge is, or as contemplation is.[1]

Now bodies seem most of all to be substantial beings, especially natural bodies, since they are the sources of all the others. Among natural bodies, some have life and others do not—by life I mean self-nourishment, growth and decay. Thus every natural body that partakes of life would be a substantial being in the third way, as a composite.[2] But since it is a certain kind of body, one that *has* life, soul would not be the same as body; for body does not exist *in* an underlying thing, but rather *as* an underlying thing and as material. Soul, then, has to be a substantial being in the second

20   way, as the form of a natural body that has life as its potency. But this kind of substantial being is being-fully-itself; so soul is the being-fully-itself of such a body. But this, again, is said in two senses, first as knowledge and second as contemplation. It is clear, then, that soul is being-fully-itself in the way knowledge is: for, in a thing to which soul belongs, there is both sleeping and being awake, and being awake is analogous to contemplating, while sleeping is analogous to having knowledge and not being at work

---

1   For example, a human being, before learning geometry, is a potential knower of geometry. One who has studied and learned geometry has taken on the form of geometrical knowledge and become fully a knower of geometry; but this human being can then be a geometrician either latently (when thinking of something else but still possessing the knowledge), or actively (when focused on a geometrical proof). Aristotle develops this distinction more fully in II.5.

2   Self-nutrition necessarily implies both the material taken as nourishment and a form that is being maintained as what it is.

with it; and in a person's development, knowledge comes first.[3] So then, soul is the *first* being-fully-itself of a natural body that has life as its potency. Such a body would be one with organs. (Even   412b the parts of plants are organs, though extremely simple: the skin protects the fruit and the leaf protects the skin; roots are analogous to mouths, since both draw in nourishment.) So if we must say what is common to every soul, it would be the first being-fully-itself of an organized natural body.[4] There is no need, therefore, to inquire whether soul and body are one, any more than whether the wax and its stamp are one, or more generally the material of each thing and that of which it is the material; "one" and "to be" are meant in a variety of ways, but being-fully-itself is their most definitive meaning.

So then, we have said what soul is universally. It is the   10 substantial being that is a thing's *logos*, or the being-what-it-is of a certain kind of body.[5] It is just as if some tool were a natural body, for example an axe: then what-it-is-to-be-an-axe would be its substantial being, and this would be its soul; bereft of this, it would no longer be an axe except in name. On the other hand, this is only an axe; the soul is not in fact the *logos* and the being-what-it-is of this kind of body, but rather of a natural body, which has its source of motion and rest in itself. We have to go on to contemplate how what has just been said applies to the parts of such a body. If, for example, the eye were an animal, vision would be its soul, since vision is the substantial being that is the eye's *logos* (or, to put it differently, an eye is the material of vision); if   20 this is lost, it is no longer an eye except in name, like a stone eye or an eye in a painting. What is true of a part must, indeed, be understood with reference to the whole of a living thing's body, since the part of perception bears the same relationship to its

---

3   Since the intellect must be actively thinking in order to attain knowledge by learning, it might seem that intellect being fully itself as thinking is prior to intellect as knowing. But the intellect most fully knows something when it reflects on it, which requires that it already have learned it.

4   The word translated "organized" is *organikos*, a word invented by Aristotle in his biological writings and the source of our "organic." The Greek word *organon* means "tool." Thus an organized body is one that has parts shaped and arranged so as to serve distinct instrumental purposes within the whole, and the body as a whole is formed as an instrument for the complex of life-activities characteristic of a particular kind of "organism".

5   See Glossary, "Being-what-it-is"

bodily part as the whole of perception bears to the whole body insofar as it is a perceptive body.[6]

413a

It is not a body that has cast off its soul that has potency to be alive, but rather one that has soul; and the seed and fruit have potency to be such a body. So then being awake, just like seeing or chopping, is its being-fully-itself, but the soul is like vision or the potency of the tool, and the body *has* the potency; but, just as the eye is both the eyeball and vision, so in this case the living thing is both the body and the soul. It is not unclear, then, that the soul is not separate from the body, or at least some parts of it are not (if it is of such a nature as to have parts), since with respect to some parts of the body it is the being-fully-itself of those same parts. But nothing prevents this being so with respect to any part of the soul that is not the being-fully-itself of anything bodily. What is still unclear, then, is whether the soul is the being-fully-itself of the body in the way the sailor is of the ship.

10

So then, as a sketch that traces the outlines around soul, let this suffice.

II.2

Out of things that are more readily apparent but unclear, what is clear and more knowable in accord with *logos* emerges. So then, we should try again to come at soul from another angle, since a delineating statement shouldn't only clarify *that* something is so (which is what most definitions tell us), but must also include and bring to light the cause. Usually the statements of definitions are like conclusions. For example: What is squaring? "Producing an equal-sided right-angled figure equal in area to a figure of unequal sides." But such a definition is a statement of the result, whereas the one that tells us that squaring is finding a mean proportional tells us the cause of the fact.[7]

20

---

6   Properly speaking, it is not the eye that perceives; rather, each part that is material for a particular kind of perception can only be such as part of a whole perceptive system of an organism, and the whole body is, from a certain point of view, material structured so as to support and be supported by a system of perception.

7   In his *Elements of Geometry*, Euclid explains the mechanics of how to construct a square with an area equal to that of a given rectilineal figure in Book 2, proposition 14. It is only after the discussion of proportionality in Book 5 that he is able to reveal (in 6.13) that this process amounts to finding a mean proportional; and this revelation gives a new clarity to the relationships within the whole class of rectilineal figures.

Let us say, then, taking it as the beginning of the inquiry, that the ensouled differs from the soulless by being alive. But since being alive is meant in several senses, we will say that something is alive if any one of these is present in it: intellect, perception, moving and stopping with regard to place, or the movement of nourishment (including both growing and withering). Hence all plants as well seem to be alive, since they clearly have within themselves a potency and a governing principle through which they continue growing and withering in opposite directions—for it is not the case that they grow only up and not down, but those that continue to nourish themselves and live toward their ends   30
grow in both (and indeed all) directions, as long as they are able to obtain nourishment. This potency can exist separately from the others, but the others cannot without this one (at least in mortal beings). This is obvious with regard to plants, since no other potency of soul is present in them.

So then, it is due to this governing principle that life belongs   413b
to living things. But something is an animal primarily due to perception, since we call things animals and not just living things if they have perception, even if they do not move or change their place. The primary kind of perception that belongs to all of them is touch; and just as the nutritive can exist separately from touch and perception as a whole, so touch can exist separately from the rest of perception. (We call "nutritive" the partial kind of soul that even plants share in.) All animals clearly have a sense of touch.

We will explain later the cause of each of these things falling   10
out as they do. For now, let us say only that the soul is the governing principle of the things mentioned (nutritive, perceptive, thinking and moving) and is bounded by them. Is each of these a soul or a part of soul—and if a part, is it such as to be separable only in *logos* or also in locus? While some of these things are not difficult to see, several involve perplexity. For, just as in the case of plants, where some cuttings clearly go on living even when separated from one another (because in the being-fully-itself of each plant its soul   20
is one, but it is potentially many), so also we see the same thing happening in other kinds of soul in the case of insects when they are cut: each of the parts has perception and motion with respect to place, and if perception then also imagination and desire (for where there is perception there is also pain and pleasure, and where these are there is necessarily appetite). The case of the intellect and the contemplative capacity is not at all clear, but it seems that this is another kind of soul and that this alone is able

to exist separately, as the eternal is from the perishable. But it is evident from these things that the remaining parts of the soul are not separable, as some claim; but that they are distinct in *logos*

30   is clear, since it is one thing to be perceptive and another to be opinion-forming (if in fact perceiving is different from opining), and likewise with each of the other aforementioned things. Moreover, to some animals all of these belong, to some only some of them, and to others only one—and this is what makes animals

414a   different. The cause of this must be investigated later. The same thing happens within the sphere of the powers of perception: some animals have them all, others some of them, others the one most necessary, touch.

That "by which" we live and perceive is meant in two ways, just like that "by which" we know (I mean knowledge and soul, since we say that we know by means of each of these), and similarly that "by which" we are healthy (either by good health or by some part of the body or the whole of it). Of these, knowledge or health

10   is a shape and a certain form, a *logos*, and a being-at-work of the thing that admits of it, i.e. of what can know or of what can be healthy (and also of what can restore health, since the being-at-work of what is responsible for making something happen seems to be present in that which is receptive and which gets disposed a certain way). The soul is that by which we live and perceive and think in the first place, so that it would be a certain *logos* and form, rather than material and the underlying thing.

As we said, substantial being is meant in three ways—as either the form, the material, or the composite of these—and of these the material is potential while the form is the being-fully-itself. And since the composite of the two is the ensouled thing, the body is not the being-fully-itself of a soul, but rather soul is the being-fully-itself of a certain body. Accordingly, those to whom

20   it seems that the soul is not a kind of body but also can not be without a body apprehend it admirably; for it is not a body, but is something of a body. Thus it exists in a body—and in a body of a specific kind, contrary to the idea of our predecessors who tried to fit it into a body without specifying in which or what kind, even though it doesn't look like random bodies admit of random things. Rather, it happens in accord with a *logos*: the being-fully-itself of each thing naturally comes to be in what has the potency for it and in the appropriate material. So then, it is evident from these things that soul is a certain being-fully-itself and *logos* of something that has the potency to be a specific kind of thing.

II.3

As we have said, in some living beings all of the potencies of soul that have been mentioned are present, in others a few, and in some only one. The potencies we spoke of were the nutritive, the perceptive, the desiring, mobility with respect to place, and the power of thought. In plants the nutritive alone is present, in other things the perceptive as well. But if the perceptive is present, so is the desiring. For desire includes appetite (as well as spiritedness and wishing); all animals have at least one of the senses, touch; and if perception is present in something, so is pleasure and pain and the pleasant and painful things; and if these are present to something so is appetite, which is desire for the pleasant thing. They certainly have perception of their food, because touch is a perception of food, since all animals nourish themselves on dry and wet and hot and cold things, and touch is the perception of these. The other senses have only an incidental role in nourishment, since sound and color and odor contribute nothing to it, and flavor is in a certain way among the things perceived by touch.[8] Hunger and thirst are appetites, the former for what is dry and warm, the latter for what is wet and cool, whereas flavor is like a sweetening for these. Later we will have to clarify these things further; for now, suffice it to say that since touch is present in animals, desire is too. The case is unclear as regards imagination, and this must be investigated later as well. In addition to these things, mobility with respect to place also belongs to some animals, and to others the power of thought and an intellect as well, namely to human beings (and anything else there may be that is similar or more worthy of honor).

So then it is clear that there would be one *logos* of soul in just the same way as there is one of geometric figure; for just as in the latter case there is no figure apart from the triangle and the others that follow in sequence, so here there is no soul apart from those mentioned. But if in addition a common *logos* were to be formulated for the figures, although it will fit all of them, it will not be the *logos* proper to any one of them; and it is the same with regard to the souls discussed. So in both cases it is ridiculous to search for a *logos* that is common to all the items but

30

414b

10

20

---

8   See below, 434b18

will never be the *logos* that is proper to any one of these beings or that corresponds to its distinct indivisible form, while neglecting to look for the latter sort.

There is also this parallel between the cases of soul and of the figures: what is prior in the sequence is always implicitly present in the other figures or ensouled things (the triangle in the rectangle, the nutritive in the perceptive). So for each being we must investigate what the soul of each is, for example what the soul of a plant is or of a human or of a beast. The cause of their being in such a sequence will have to be investigated.[9] For the perceptive does not exist without the nutritive, but the nutritive exists apart from the perceptive in plants. And again, none of the other senses is present without the sense of touch, but touch is present without the others, since many animals have neither sight nor hearing nor sense of smell. And some of the perceptive beings have mobility with respect to place, while others do not. The most complete and fewest in number have reasoning and thinking; and in those in which reasoning exists of perishable beings, all the rest exist too, while reasoning does not exist in all those that have all the rest. Some are not even endowed with imagination, while others live relying on that alone. With regard to contemplative intellect there is a different *logos*. So then it is clear that the *logos* that renders account of each of these is also the one most proper to render account of soul.

II.4

One who is going to investigate these things must grasp what each of them is, and after that inquire further in this way about what is directly connected to them and about the rest. But if one is to say what each of them is (the power of thought, the perceptive power or the nutritive), one must rather first say what thinking is and what perceiving is; for in the order of *logos*, the forms of being-at-work and the actions are prior to the potencies for them. But if so, and if prior to these one must have contemplated their objects, then for the same reason one ought first to delineate the latter, i.e. nutriment and the perceptible and the intelligible.

So then first one must speak of nutrition and reproduction. For the nutritive soul belongs already to all the others; it is the first and most common potency of soul, the one through which living belongs to all things. Its works are reproduction and the

---

9   III.12-13

use of food. For one of the most natural of works for living things (as many as are complete and not damaged, or not spontaneously generating) is to make another like itself—an animal an animal, a plant a plant—so as to partake so far as it is able in the eternal and divine. All things reach for this, and for the sake of this do whatever they do according to nature ("for the sake of" being twofold: *for* what is aimed at and *for* what is benefitted). Since, then, it is unable to share in the eternal and divine by way of continuity, because perishable things do not admit of persisting as the same thing and one in number, each thing shares in the way in which it is able to partake (one more, another less). So it persists not as the same thing but as one like itself, not one in number but one in form.

415b

The soul is a cause and a governing principle of the living body. But these things may be meant in various ways; and likewise the soul is a cause in three distinct ways. The soul is a cause as the origin of motion, as that for the sake of which, and as the substantial being of ensouled bodies.[10] That it is as substantial being is clear: the substantial being is the cause of the being of each thing, living is the being of living things, and soul is the cause and governing principle of these. Furthermore, the *logos* of what has being in potential is its being-fully-itself.

10

It is also evident that the soul is the cause as that for the sake of which. For just as the intellect acts for the sake of something, nature acts in the same way; and this something is its end.[11] The soul is such a thing in living things according to nature. For all natural bodies are instruments of the soul (those of plants just as well as those of animals), as being for the sake of soul. It is that for the sake of which in two ways: both what is aimed at and what is benefitted.

20

And indeed, soul is also that from which motion in place originates. Although this potency does not belong to all living things, alteration and growth also exist by way of soul; for perception seems to be some kind of alteration, and nothing perceives that does not also partake in soul. It is likewise in the

---

10   In *Physics* II.3, Aristotle distinguishes the four ways in which something can be called a cause, or an explanation of the "why" of something. (See Glossary, "Cause".) The fourth way is as material, and this is the only way in which soul is not the cause of a living thing's being what it is: although it is responsible for the ordering of the material, it is not itself material.

11   *Physics* II.8 explains why this does not require attributing conscious purposes to all natural beings.

case of growth and withering: nothing withers or grows naturally without nourishing itself, and nothing nourishes itself that does not share in life. Empedocles did not speak properly in this regard, when he posited that when plants extend their roots downward,

416a this growth occurs due to earth's tending this way by nature, and upward growth similarly on account of fire. He did not even understand up and down properly. For up and down are not the same for all things as they are for the whole cosmos; but as the head is for animals, so the roots are for plants, if one ought to call organs the same or different by the works they do. Besides, what is it that holds together the fire and earth that are tending in opposite directions? For it will be separated out, if there is not going to be something preventing it; and if there is going to be, this will be soul, which is the cause of its growing and nourishing itself.

10   To some, the cause of nourishment and growth seems simply to be the nature of fire, for it alone of the bodies or elements manifestly nourishes itself and grows. Thus one might take this to be what is acting both in plants and in animals. However, while it is in some way a co-cause, it is not the cause simply, but rather soul is. For the growth of fire is without limit, as long as there is fuel; but of all things composed by nature there is a limit and a *logos* of size and growth—and these things are characteristic of soul but not of fire, and of *logos* rather than of material.

20   Since the same potency of the soul is nutritive and reproductive, it is necessary first to draw distinctions concerning nutriment, for it is by this work that this potency distinguishes itself from the other ones. Now, opposite seems to be nutriment for opposite—not every one for every opposite, but only those that have not only their coming-to-be but also their growth from each other. For many things come to be from each other; but (as in the case of what is healthy coming to be from what is ailing) not all are quantitative. And of those that are, not all seem to be nutriment in the same way for each other, but water is nourishment for fire whereas fire does not nourish water. It seems to be most of all the case in the simple elemental bodies that one nourishes and the other is nourished.

30   But this does involve a perplexity. For some say that like is nourished by like, just as it is augmented. But to others it seems the other way, just as we were saying, that opposite is nourished by opposite; for like is unaffected by like, whereas nutriment changes and is digested (and for all things, change is into what is opposite or in between). Besides, food has something done to it by the one who feeds on it, but not the feeder by the food—just as it is not the carpenter who has something done to him by the material, but rather the reverse, while the carpenter only changes   416b from inactivity to being-at-work. It makes a difference, however, whether the nutriment is what is incorporated at the end or at the beginning. If it is both, but in the one case digested and in the other undigested, then nutriment may be spoken of in both ways: for when it is undigested, opposite is being nourished by opposite, but when digested, then it is like by like. It is clear, then, that both sides speak in a way correctly and in a way not correctly. So since nothing nourishes itself that does not share in life, what nourishes itself would be the ensouled body, as ensouled; thus nutriment is   10 relative to what is ensouled—and not merely incidentally.

Moreover, what it is to be nourishing differs from what it is to be augmenting: it is augmentative insofar as the ensouled thing has quantity, while it is nourishment insofar as the ensouled thing is a distinct something and a substantial being—for it preserves the substantial being, which exists only so long as it continues to nourish itself. But it is also productive, generating not the thing that nourishes itself, but another like the thing that nourishes itself; for its substantial being already exists, and a thing does not generate itself, but preserves itself. Hence this kind of governing principle of the soul is a potency of the sort to preserve, as the kind of thing it is, the being that admits of it; and nutriment provides for its being at work, so that, deprived of nutriment, a thing cannot exist.

Since there are three things involved (that which is nourished, that by which it is nourished, and that which does the nourishing),   20 what does the nourishing is the *first* soul, what is nourished is the body that has this, and that by which it is nourished is the nutriment. Since it is right to assign every thing its name from its end, and its end is to generate something like itself, the first soul would be that which is generative of something like itself. "That by which it is nourished," however, is meant two ways, just as that by which one steers is both the hand and the rudder: the former is both mover and moved, while the latter is only moved. All nutriment must be able to be digested, and digestion works by way of heat; hence every ensouled thing has heat.

So then, what nutriment is has been said in outline. It will have   30 to be further clarified later in discourses devoted specifically to it.[12]

---

12   Given that he has identified the nutritive power with the generative, Aristotle may have in mind his *Generation of Animals*. Remarks in Chapter 3 of *On Sleep and Waking* (456b5-6) suggest that he treated digestion more extensively in a work now lost to us.

II.5

Having delineated these things, let us give an account common to all perception. As was said before, perception involves being moved and undergoing something, since it seems to be some
35 kind of alteration. Some say it is a case of like being affected by
417a like. This is in a way possible and in a way impossible, as we have said in the general discussions concerning acting and being acted upon.[13] But if the senses themselves contain fire and earth and the other elements, and if perception is of these as such or of what is incidental to them, it is perplexing why there is no perception of the senses themselves, and why they do not produce perception without external things. It is clear, then, that the perceptive power exists not as a being-at-work, but only as a potency. Thus it does not perceive just as the combustible does not itself burn on its own without something to ignite it, for otherwise it ought to ignite itself and have no need of fire that is already fully-itself.
10   But since we use the word "perceiving" in two senses—for we say that someone with a potency of hearing and seeing is "hearing" and "seeing" (even one who happens to be asleep), as well as the one who is already at work—perception would also be meant in two ways, as a potency and as at-work. Likewise, being perceived has existence both as potential and as at-work. In the first place, then, we speak of the same being as being acted upon or moved and being at work, for motion is a kind of being-at-work, though incomplete, as has been said in other places.[14] But, on the other hand, all things are acted upon and moved by what already is at work and productive of motion. So then it is the case that, on the one hand, a thing is acted upon by its like, and on the other, it is acted upon by the unlike, just
20 as we said: the unlike is acted upon, but once acted upon it is like.[15]

---

13   Perhaps Aristotle refers to *On Generation and Corruption* I.7, where he raises in more general terms the difficulty he is about to discuss.

14   *Physics* III.1-2

15   This is a difficult but crucial point. Aristotle is trying to break us out of our tendency to think of occurrences in simplistically material and mechanistic terms. The change that occurs when perception takes place cannot be adequately grasped simply in terms of bodily motions, since imagining them this way remains wholly outside the actual phenomenon of perception. What is perception if not an experience? The real being of perception *as perception* is the experience of a potency being set to work by that which is able to be perceived. The perceptive power becomes like the object in two ways: by being brought into action by that which is acting upon it and by (in a certain respect) becoming the thing it perceives. It can go from unlike to like because it already exists as a potency that is oriented toward becoming like its object. Thus it is not the kind of thing that can be perceived or set itself in motion.

It is necessary, however, to make some distinctions with respect to potency and being-fully-itself, for we are speaking of them now in a simple way. For in one way something is a knower in the way that we would say a human being is a knower, because a human being is one of the things that are able to know and to have knowledge. In another way we say that someone who is literate is now a knower. Each of the two is capable, but not in the same way: one is because he is of a certain kind and is the right material, the other because he is capable of contemplating when he wishes, if nothing external prevents him. The one who is already contemplating is being fully what he is, and (in the definitive sense of the word) is a knower of this A. Both of the first two are knowers with respect to their potency; but the first has been altered through learning and through changing repeatedly out of the contrary condition, while the second changes by going from having perception or literacy that is not at work to being at work in another way.

30

417b

Being acted upon is not a simple thing either. In one sense it is a certain destruction of something by its opposite; in another sense it is the preservation of what has being as a potency by what has being as fully itself and is like it (i.e. like it in the way that potency stands toward being-fully-itself). For when what has knowledge comes to be contemplating, it is either not a case of being altered (since it is an elevation of the same thing into being-fully-itself) or it is some other kind of alteration. Hence it is not proper to say that a thinking being is altered when it thinks, nor a house-builder when he is building. Thus, in the case of what thinks and reflects, what causes the change from being as potency to being-fully-itself ought rightly to be given some name other than "instruction." For, when something goes from being as a potency to learning and receiving knowledge from the one whose being is fully-itself and able to instruct, then it must be said either that it is not acted upon or that there are two modes of alteration (as was said): one a change toward a negative condition, and the other toward a thing's nature and proper dispositions.

10

The initial change in the perceiving being comes about from its progenitor; once it is generated, it already has perception, in the manner in which one possesses knowledge. Its being-at-work has been said to be like contemplating, but it differs in that the things productive of its being-at-work are external (the visible, the audible, and likewise with the rest of the perceptibles). The cause of the difference is that perception at work is of particulars, but

20

knowledge is of universals, which in some way are in the soul. Thus, one can think on one's own when one wishes, but one cannot perceive on one's own, since something perceptible must be present—which holds true even of sciences that are of perceptible things, and for the same reason: perceptibles are among the things that are particular and external.

Making clarifications about these, however, would be for another occasion.[16] For now, let this much be delineated: that since "in potential" is not meant simply, but in one way we might say that a child has potential to be a general, while in the other way we would say this of a grown man, this second is the way the perceptive power has it. The difference between the two is without a name, so even though *that* they are different and *how* they are different has been delineated, it is still necessary to use "being acted upon" and "being altered" as standard names. The perceptive power is potentially such as the perceptible thing already is fully, as has been said. So then it is acted upon when it is unlike, but once it has been acted upon it has become similar and is such as that thing is.

II.6

With regard to each sense, one must speak of the things perceived first. But "what is perceived" is meant in three ways, two of which we say are perceived in virtue of themselves, and the other one only incidentally. Of the first two, one is proper to each sense and the other is common to them all. By "proper" I mean that which is not able to be perceived by another sense, and concerning which it is impossible to be deceived (vision of color, hearing of sound, taste of flavor). While touch has a great variety of objects, still each sense judges what is proper to it and is not deceived about whether it is color or sound, but about what the colored thing is or where, or what or where the sounding thing is. It is such things that are called "proper" to each sense; the things called "common" are motion, rest, number, figure and magnitude, since such things are not proper to any one of them, but common to all. For a certain motion is perceptible to both touch and sight. "Incidentally sensible" are such things as whether the white thing is the son of Diares; this is incidentally sensible because the thing of which there is perception is related only incidentally to the white that is perceived. Hence nothing is acted upon by the thing

30

418a

10

20

---

16   Aristotle has more to say on these topics in III.3 and III.7-8.

sensible in this way as such. Of the things perceived in virtue of themselves, the proper ones are sensible in the definitive way, and it is toward these that the distinct being of each sense is naturally ordered.

II.7

That toward which sight is ordered is, then, the visible. The visible is in the first place color, and also something else of which an account can be given in speech but which happens to have no name. (What we are speaking of will be quite clear in what follows.)

What is visible is color. It is what is on things visible in themselves—"in themselves" not in a logical sense, but because they have in themselves the cause of being visible. All color is able to set into motion that of which the being-at-work is transparency; this is its nature. Hence it is not visible without light, but every color of each thing is seen in light. Thus something must first be said about light.

There is something that is transparent. I call transparent that which, although it is visible, is not simply speaking visible in virtue of itself but rather because of the color of something else. Such is air and water and a great number of solid bodies; it is not, however, *as* air or *as* water that it is transparent, but rather because there is a certain nature present that is the same in both (and also in the eternal body on high). Light is the being-at-work of this thing, of the transparent as transparent; and darkness is present in what is potentially transparent. Light is, as it were, the color of the transparent itself, whenever the transparent is fully-itself because of fire or something like it, such as a body on high (for something that is one and the same belongs also to this).[17]

So then what the transparent is has been said and also what light is, because it is not fire or body more generally nor an "outflowing" from any body (which itself would just be a body of the same kind), but rather the being-present of fire or some such thing in the transparent. For it is not possible for two bodies to be in the same place at once. Furthermore, light seems to be the contrary of darkness; but darkness seems to be the removal of such a disposition from what is transparent, so that clearly the

30

418b

10

20

---

17   Because Aristotle thought that the stars and planets were made of some bright and imperishable material, he thought this had to be something unchangeable, unlike fire, but possessing the same luminous character. He called it *aether*.

being-present of this is light. Empedocles, or anyone else who has said the same, is incorrect to say that light travels and at a certain time stretches out between the earth and the outer circumference without our noticing it. This contradicts both the appearances and the clarity of reason; for, while it might escape our notice over a small interval, it is too much to ask us to believe that it does so in traveling from the rising-point to the western horizon.

It is the colorless that admits color, and the soundless that admits sound. The colorless is the transparent and the invisible or barely visible, such as the dark seems to be; but this is just the

30   transparent, not when it is fully-itself as transparent, but when it is potentially so, for it is the same nature that is at one time darkness and at another time light.

419a   Not all visible things, however, are in light, but only the proper color of each thing. For some things are not seen in the light, but produce perception in darkness, such as things that appear flame-like and glowing (there is not a single name for them), lichen, horn, the heads, scales and eyes of fish—but one does not see the color proper to any of these. Through what cause these things are seen is for another discussion.

For now, this much is clear: what is seen in light is color. Thus

10   it is not seen without light, for the very being of color is to be what can move the transparent into being-at-work, and the being-fully-itself of the transparent is light. Here is a clear indication of this: when someone puts something that has color onto the eye itself, it is not seen; rather, color sets in motion the transparent (air for example), and by being in contact with this the sense organ is moved. Democritus, then, does not speak well when he opines that, if the intermediate space were entirely emptied, it would even be possible to see an ant in the heavens clearly. This is impossible. For seeing occurs when the sense organ is being acted upon in some way, and it cannot be by the color itself that is seen, so it

20   must be by the medium, and thus it is necessary for there to be a medium. If it is emptied out, a thing will not be seen clearly; rather, it will not be seen at all.

Why color has to be seen in light has been stated. Fire is seen in both darkness and light, of necessity, since by it the transparent becomes transparent. It is the same story for sound and odor: nothing that touches the sense organ produces perception of them. Rather, by sound or odor the medium is moved, and by this each of the sense organs is moved, so that whenever someone places a sounding or odorous thing upon the organ itself it does

not produce any perception. It holds similarly for touch and taste,   30
though it does not seem so; the cause of this will be clear later.[18]
The medium of sound is air. The medium of odor is without a
name, for it is some characteristic common to air and water; for
as the transparent is to color, so what is present in both of these
is to what has odor. For aquatic animals seem to have a sense of   419b
smell, but human beings and as many land animals as breathe are
unable to smell without breathing. The cause of these things will
also be told later.[19]

II.8

Now, however, let us first make some distinctions concerning
sound and hearing. Sound is twofold: in its being-at-work, and in
potential. For we say that some things do not even have a sound,
such as a sponge or wool, and that others do, such as bronze or
whatever is hard and smooth, because it is capable of making
sound—i.e. causing sound to be at work between itself and the
sense of hearing.

When sound comes to be at work, it is always from something   10
in relation to something (as well as in something). For it is a
striking that produces it, so that it is impossible for sound to come
about when there is only one thing, since the thing striking and
the thing struck are different. Thus the thing sounding sounds in
relation to something, and the striking does not occur without
motion.

As we said, though, sound is not the striking of just anything
whatever. One does not produce a sound by striking wool, but
rather bronze and things that are smooth and hollow—bronze
because it is smooth, while hollow things produce many strikings
after the first one because of the reverberation (since what is set in
motion is unable to get out).

Moreover, it is heard in air, and also (though less) in water;
but it is not air or water that is responsible for sound. Rather, it is
necessary for a striking to occur of solid things in relation to one   20
another or in relation to the air. The latter happens when the air
resists the striking and is not dissipated: whenever it is quickly
and forcefully struck, it sounds. The motion of the striking thing
must be faster than the dispersion of the air—as if one were trying
to strike a heap or swirl of sand as it rapidly passed by.

---

18   II.10-11
19   II.9, 421b9-26

An echo occurs whenever the air is bounced back again by a mass of air that has been unified by a cavity circumscribing it and preventing it from dispersing, as if it were a ball. And it seems that echo is always occurring, though not distinctly. For what happens with sound is just like what happens with light: light is always

30 being reflected (otherwise there would not be light everywhere, but rather darkness outside of direct sunlight), but since it is not reflected so well as from water or bronze or some other smooth thing, it produces shadow, by which light is distinguished.[20]

It is rightly said that the "void" is responsible for hearing; for the air appears to be void, and it is what produces hearing whenever it is moved as one continuous thing. Because of its loose

420a consistency, however, this only happens when the thing struck is smooth: since the surface of the smooth thing is one, the air becomes one along with it.

A sounding thing, then, is one that moves a single body of air in its continuity up to the organ of hearing. The organ of hearing is in its nature continuous with the air. Because it is in the air, when the external air is moved the internal is moved too. Thus the animal does not hear with every part, nor does air flow through it everywhere, since not even the part that is ensouled so as to be set in motion by sound has air throughout it.

The air itself is soundless, since it is easily dispersed; but when it is prevented from being dispersed, the movement of it is sound.

10 The air in the ears is walled in to keep it motionless, so that one can hear accurately all the differences of the motion. Hence we can also hear in water, since, because of the ear's spirals, the water does not get into it and penetrate the air that is conjoined with its nature. If that does happen, it cannot hear; nor can it when the ear drum is damaged (just like the surface of the eye). But it is also an indication of its hearing or not hearing that there is a constant echoing in the ear, like in a shell; for the air in the ears is always moving with its own motion, whereas a *sound* is from elsewhere and not its own. On this account some say that hearing is by means of the empty and echoing, because we hear by means of air that is bounded and contained.

20 But which is the one that sounds: the thing struck or the thing striking? Or is it rather both, but in different ways? For the sound is a motion of something capable of being moved in just the way

---

20   That is, we recognize where direct light is by contrast with what is indirectly lit and shadowy.

that something rebounds off a smooth surface when someone hits it. As has been said, it is not every struck and striking thing that sounds, for example when a needle hits a needle. What is struck must be an even surface, so that the air rebounds and vibrates as one mass.

The differences of sounds become clear in the sound when it is at work; for just as without light colors are not seen, without sound there is no sharp and flat. These are named by a metaphor from tangibles: the sharp moves the sense a lot in a short time, **30** while the flat in a long time moves it little. It is not that the sharp is fast nor the flat slow, but the former comes to be as it is from the swiftness of the motion, and the latter from its slowness. The **420b** analogy seems to be with sharp and blunt in regard to touch, for what is sharp stabs and what is blunt presses, since the former produces its motion in a short time, the latter in a long one. Thus it is incidental that one is fast and the other slow.

So then, concerning sound, let it be so delineated. Voice, however, is a certain ensouled sound; for, though none of the soulless things is vocal, yet they are said to have voices through a likeness. For example, the flute and lyre and other such soulless things have range, melody and articulation, and voice seems to have these also. Many of the animals do not have voice, such as the **10** bloodless ones, and among blooded ones the fishes. The ones said to have voice (such as those in the Achelous[21]) make sound with their gills or some other such thing.

Voice is the sound of an animal, and not just of any part whatsoever. But since everything sounds from something striking something, and also in something, which is air, then it stands to reason that only those things that take in air would have voice. Nature, indeed, uses the breath that is drawn for two works—just as the tongue is used for both taste and articulation, of which the first (taste) is necessary (which is why it belongs to many animals), while expressing meaning is for the sake of living well. So also **20** breathing is used because it is necessary for the internal heat (the cause of which will be discussed elsewhere[22]) and also with a view to voice, so as to provide for living well. The throat is an instrument of breathing, and so it is a part that exists for the sake of the lungs, by means of which land-animals have more heat than

---

21   The Achelous is a river in northwestern Greece that divides the Acarnanian and Aetolian regions. It is not known what kind of fish Aristotle refers to here.

22   *On Respiration* 1-10

the others. The part that has the principal need of inbreathed air is the area around the heart; thus the air breathed in necessarily enters the animal's interior. So the striking of the air against what is called the windpipe, brought about by the soul that is in these parts, is voice.

30 But not every sound of an animal is voice, as we said (for one can make sound with the tongue, or in imitation of those who cough). Rather, the striking thing must be ensouled and must have a share in some kind of imagination, for voice is a kind of sound that signifies, and not merely an effect of the inbreathed
421a air, as a cough is. Rather, it uses this air to strike the air in the windpipe against the windpipe itself. An indication of this is the inability to give voice while one is breathing in or out; it is only possible when holding the breath, since the one who is holding it puts it in motion. So it is also clear why fish are voiceless: they have no larynx. They lack this part because they do not take in air or breathe it. Through what cause, though, is for a different discourse.[23]

II.9

Regarding smell and what is smelled, matters are not so easily distinguished as with the other senses; for it is not as clear what sort of thing smell is as it is in the case of sound or light or color.
10 The reason is that we do not have precision in this sense, but are inferior to many animals. The human being smells poorly, and does not smell anything that is odorous unaccompanied by the painful or the pleasant, since the sense organ is imprecise. It is reasonable to say that animals with hard eyes perceive color this way, and that the differences of the colors are not entirely clear to them outside of the ones that do or do not occasion fear; this is also the way the human race is with respect to smells. This sense seems to bear an analogy to taste (and similarly the forms of flavor to those of odor). But we have a more precise sense of taste because
20 it is a kind of touch, which is a sense that is extremely precise in humans. In the other senses humans fall behind many of the animals, but with respect to touch they discriminate far better than the others. Hence they are also the most intelligent of the animals. An indication of this is that the human race divides into the naturally well endowed and the naturally unendowed based on this sense organ rather than any other: the tough-skinned are

---

23 *Parts of Animals* III.6, 669a1-5, and *On Respiration* 15, 474b25-475a11

naturally lacking in thinking, while the soft-skinned are naturally well-endowed.

Just as one taste is sweet and another bitter, so it is with smells. But, while in some cases the odor and the taste are analogous (I mean, for example, sweetness of smell and sweet flavor), in other cases they are opposite. Similarly, odor is pungent, harsh, sharp or oily. But just as we said, since odors, just like tastes, are not especially clear, they have taken their names from the latter because of the similarity of the things (for example, sweetness is the odor of saffron and honey, and pungency the odor of thyme and such things; and it is the same in other cases). Smell is also like hearing and each of the other senses in that, just as hearing is of the audible as well as the inaudible, and vision of the visible and invisible, so also smell is of the odorous and inodorous. The inodorous is, first, that which is entirely incapable of having odor, and second, that which has scant or negligible odor; and one speaks similarly of the tasteless.

The sense of smell also occurs through a medium, like air or water, since even aquatic animals (whether they are blooded or bloodless) seem to perceive smell, just like those that are in air; for many of them as well are guided to their food from far away entirely by its smell. Hence arises a perplexity, as to whether all animals smell in the same way. The human being, for one, smells when inhaling, but not when exhaling or holding the breath, neither from far nor near nor even if putting something inside the nostril itself. (It is common to all animals that a thing placed on the sense organ is not sensed, but the inability to sense without inhaling is a feature of human beings, as is clear to those who test it.) The bloodless animals, then, since they do not inhale, would have some other kind of sense than the ones discussed. But that is not possible, if they perceive odor, since the perception of an odorous thing with respect to both good smells and bad is the sense of smell. Besides, they seem to be destroyed by the same powerful smells as humans are, such as bitumen and brimstone and things of that sort. They must, then, perceive smell, but without inhaling.

For humans, this sense organ seems to differ from that of other animals just as the eyes do from those of hard-eyed animals. Those that have lids as protection (like a sheath) do not see if they do not move them or draw them back, whereas the hard-eyed have no such thing but simply see what comes about in the transparent. So for some animals the organ of smell is uncovered, like the eyes, while those that take in air have coverings that uncover it when

30

421b

10

20

422a

they breathe in and their vessels and passageways dilate. Because of this, things that inhale do not smell in the wet, since they have to smell when inhaling and they cannot do this in the wet. Odor is of the dry (just as flavor is of the wet), and the organ of smell is potentially this way.[24]

II.10

The tasteable is something tangible of a sort, and this is the cause of its not being perceptible through the medium of some other bodily being, since touch is not either. Furthermore, the body in which there is flavor, which is the tasteable thing, is in the wet as its material, which is something tangible. Thus, even if we were in water, we would perceive a sweetness that was introduced into it; but the sensation would not come to us through a medium, but by its mixture with the wet, just as in the case of drinking. (Color, on the contrary, is not seen this way, i.e. by being mixed, nor by means of effluences.) So then there is nothing that serves as medium; but as color is what is visible, so flavor is what is tasteable. Nothing produces the sensation of flavor without moisture, but something can possess moisture at work or in potential, such as the salty, which is easily dissolved itself and also produces liquid when joined with the tongue.

Vision is of both the visible and the invisible (since darkness is invisible, but vision also discriminates this), and moreover of the exceedingly bright (since this too is invisible, though in a different way than darkness); and likewise hearing is of both sound and silence (the former audible, the latter not audible), and is also of loud sound just as vision is of the bright (for just as a tiny sound is inaudible, so too in a way is a great and violent one). In one case it is called invisible absolutely, just as in other matters one speaks of the impossible; in the other case, one calls invisible what is of a nature to be visible but does not have visibility, or barely does, just as one speaks of something limbless or seedless. In just this way, taste is of the tasteable as well as the untasteable, the latter either having little or negligible flavor or being destructive of the sense of taste. The drinkable and undrinkable seems to be a fundamental starting point, for there is some sense of taste with respect to both; but the latter is bad and destructive of the sense of taste, while the former is in accord with nature. But drinking belongs jointly to touch and taste.

---

24   Cf. *On Sensation* 5, 443a1-b14

Since the tasteable is wet, it is necessary for its sense organ   422b
to be neither fully itself something moist nor incapable of being
moistened. For the sense of taste is affected in some way by the
tasteable, as tasteable. What is required, then, is the moistening
of something capable of becoming moist while still preserving its
capacity, but something that is not itself moist—and this is the sense
organ of taste. An indication of this is that when it is completely
dry the tongue does not perceive, nor when it is excessively wet.
(Such sustained contact with a prior moistness occurs whenever
someone who has already tasted a strong flavor tastes another, or
when, for example, all things appear bitter to the sick because they
perceive with a tongue full of such moisture.)

The forms of flavor, like those of color, are, in the simple   10
instances, contraries: the sweet and the bitter. Then bordering on
the former is the oily, and on the latter the salty; and between these
are the pungent, the harsh, the sour and the sharp. These seem to
be pretty much the differences of flavors. So then, what is able to
taste is what is potentially such a thing, and what is tasteable by it
is what can bring about its being-fully-itself.

II.11

One same account comprehends both the tangible and touch,
for if touch is not one sense but many, then the tangible sensibles
are also many. Whether they are one or many involves perplexity.
So too does the question what the sense organ of the tangible   20
is, i.e. whether the flesh is (and what is analogous in the other
animals), or whether it serves instead as the medium, while the
primary sense organ is something else inside.

Now, every sense seems to be of some one opposition. For
example, sight is of white and black, hearing of sharp and flat,
taste of bitter and sweet. In touch, however, are included many
oppositions: hot/cold, dry/moist, hard/soft, and others of this sort.
As regards this perplexity, however, there is some mitigation in the
fact that even for the other senses there are several oppositions. For
example, in voice there is not only sharpness and flatness, but also   30
greatness and smallness and smoothness and roughness of voice
and other such things. Regarding color, too, there are other such
differences. But what the single underlying thing is that serves for
touch as sound does for hearing is not clear.

Concerning whether the sense organ is internal or is instead   423a
immediately the flesh, the fact that the sensing arises at the same
time that contacts are made is no sure indication. For even if one

were to make something like a membrane and wrap it around the flesh, the sensation would still communicate itself immediately upon being touched. It is quite clear, however, that the sense organ is not in this thing; and if it came to be naturally conjoined, the sensation would penetrate even faster. Hence this part of the body seems to be in the same condition as the air would if it were naturally conjoined to us all around; for then we would seem to perceive sound and color and smell with some one thing, and vision, hearing and smell would seem to be some single kind of sensation. As it is, though, through their being distinct from that in which the motions occur, what are called the sense organs are manifested as being different. Regarding touch, however, this is still unclear, for the ensouled body cannot be composed of water or air, since it has to be something solid. What remains is for it to be mixed of earth and these things, as flesh and what is analogous to it tends to be. Thus the very body must be naturally grown as a medium of that which has the power of touch, through which the multitude of sensations occurs. The case of the tongue makes it clear that they are multiple, since the same part perceives all the tangibles as well as flavor. So then if the rest of the flesh perceived flavor, taste and touch would seem to be one and the same sense; as it is, however, they are two, since they do not interchange.[25]

One might, though, be perplexed by the following, since every body has depth (which is its third magnitude). When some intermediate body is between two bodies, they are not permitted to touch one another. But what is moist is not without a body, nor what is wet, but it must be water or have water. When, however, things touch each other in the water, since their extremities are not dry, they necessarily have water in between, which coats their edges. If this is true, then one thing cannot touch another in water. But it is the same way in the air as well (for the air is disposed toward the things in it like the water is to the things in that water, but this goes unnoticed by us, just as the animals in the water do

---

25   Since every part of the body (other than the hair and nails, which are outgrowths of excess material) is sensitive to tangibles, it is the whole body and not just the outer skin that serves as medium for touch— including the bodily parts that also serve as organs for other, more localized senses. This observation, along with the suggestion that the other sense organs themselves also serve as media for the sensations they are organized for, begins to raise the question what exactly it is that receives and perceives sensations, and thus prepares for the discussion of a central sensing capacity and the integration of the various senses in III.2. (In *On Sensation*, 439a1-2, Aristotle reasons that this integration of sensations takes place in the heart.)

not notice if something wet is touched by something wet). So then,   423b
is the perception of all things similar in manner, or is it differently
of different things, just as it now seems that taste and touch are by
contact, while the others are from afar?

This, however, is not the case, but we perceive even the hard
and the soft through other things, just like the sounding and the
visible and the odorous—except that the latter are far off and the
former are close up, so that it is not noticed. We perceive all things
through their medium, but in the former cases it goes unnoticed.
Indeed, just as we said earlier, even if we perceived all the tangibles
through a membrane without noticing that it intervened, we   10
would be disposed just as we are now in the water and in the air;
for as it is now, it seems to us that we touch them and that there is
nothing in between.

But the tangible differs from the visible and the sounding, in
that we perceive the latter through the medium's doing something
to us, whereas we perceive the tangibles not under the influence of
the medium but along with the medium, like a man who is struck
through his shield: for it is not the case that the shield, having been
struck, subsequently banged into the man, but rather both ended
up being struck at the same time together. On the whole, then,
as the air and water are situated for seeing, hearing and smell, so
the flesh and the tongue seem to be situated for the sense organ
of each of them. If its sense organ were touched immediately, in   20
neither case would sensation occur, just as if someone were to
place a white body on the surface of the eye. In this way, too, it is
clear that the sense organ of the tangible is internal, since the same
might happen as for the others: things placed upon the sense organ
are not perceived, but things placed upon the flesh are perceived,
hence flesh is the medium of the tangible.

Tangibles, then, are the differences of body as body (I mean
the differences that distinguish the elements—hot/cold, dry/
moist—about which we have spoken previously in the discussions
of the elements[26]). The sense organ is what is receptive to the feel   30
of these, and is that in which what is called the sense of touch
primarily resides, the part that is such in potential. To perceive is   424a
to be acted upon in some way; so the thing making it be like itself
is at work, and it makes the other thing, which is potentially such,
to be such. Hence we do not perceive what is equally as hot or
cold or hard or soft as ourselves, but only the excesses, inasmuch

26   *On Generation and Corruption*, II.2-3

as the sense is like a kind of mean of the opposition that is in the sensibles. It is through this that it discriminates the sensibles; for the intermediate is able to discriminate, since it becomes either extreme in relation to the other. Just as what is going to perceive white and black must be neither of them actively, but potentially
10   both (and thus also in the other cases), so also in the case of touch it must be neither hot nor cold.

Moreover, just as it turned out that vision was somehow of both the visible and the invisible (and it was likewise for the rest of the oppositions as well), so also touch is of the tangible and the intangible. And the intangible is both what, being among the tangibles, has to a very small degree a difference that belongs to tangible things (as is the case with air), and also what has the excesses of what is tangible, as destructive things do.

So then, an account has been given in outline for each of the senses.

II.12

Universally, however, concerning every sense, one must understand that the sense is that which is receptive of the sensible forms without the material, as wax receives the seal of the signet-
20   ring without the iron or gold: if it takes a gold or bronze seal, it does so not insofar as the seal is gold or bronze. Likewise, the sense is acted upon by each of the things having color or flavor or sound, but not in virtue of what each of them is said to be, but insofar as it is such-like, and in accord with a *logos*. The sense organ is that in which primarily this sort of potency exists. In one way, then, they are the same thing, but their being is different: the perceiving thing would be some kind of magnitude, while certainly what it is to be perceptive is not a magnitude, nor is the sense; rather, it is some *logos* and potency of the magnitude it belongs to.

From these things it is also evident why the excesses of
30   the sensibles destroy the sense organs: whenever the motion overpowers the sense organ, the *logos* that is the perception is ruined, just like the harmony and tone of strings too violently banged.[27] It is clear too why plants do not perceive, although they have a certain part of soul and are somehow affected by the things
424b   that are tangible to them (for they get cold and warm). The cause

---

27   Here, in keeping with the musical analogy, "*logos*" is meant primarily in the sense of mathematical ratio, but secondarily in the sense of distinctly articulated form.

is that they do not have a mean, nor such a principle as is able to receive the forms of sensible things, but are only affected along with the material.

One might be perplexed as to whether something could be affected by odor if it is unable to smell, or by color if it is unable to see, and similarly in the case of the others. But if odor is that which is smelly, then odor as such, if it produces anything, produces smell; so nothing that is incapable of smelling is able to be affected by odor. The account is the same for the other cases: none of the things capable of perception can be acted upon except in the respect in which each is perceptive. This is clear as well in the following way. It is not light and darkness nor sound nor odor that affect a body; rather, it is the things in which these are (for example, it is the air that accompanies the thunder that splits the wood). But the tangibles and flavors do have an effect—otherwise what would it be that soulless things are affected and altered by? So then, do the other sensible qualities also produce an effect, or is it not every body that is able to be affected by smell and sound, while those that are acted upon are indeterminate and not abiding, such as air? For air gets smelly, as if it is being affected in some way; and what is it to smell, if not to be affected in some way? Or is it rather that to smell is to perceive, whereas the air that is affected suddenly becomes something perceptible?[28]

10

---

28   In this summary chapter of the discussion of the senses, Aristotle shows how far his reflections have taken us from the simplistic materialism of his predecessors who explained sensing in terms of elements recognizing their own like. It is not an indeterminate body (like air) that can smell, but rather a body suitably formed of suitable material so as to receive the sensible forms communicated through a particular material medium.

Book Three

III.1

22   One might be confident that there is not another sense beside the five (by which I mean vision, hearing, smell, taste and touch) based on the following. If we currently have perception of everything for which the sense is touch (for all the affections of the tangible as tangible are perceptible to us by means of touch); and it is necessary that, lacking some sense, we will also lack some sense organ; and however many things we perceive by touching them ourselves are perceptible by touch, which is a sense we happen to

30   have, while however many we perceive through a medium without touching the things themselves we perceive by means of simple bodies (I mean such as air and water); and it is the case that, on the one hand, when multiple sensibles that are different in kind from one another are perceived through one of these simple media, a being having a sense organ of that kind is necessarily able to perceive both (for example, if the sense organ is of air, and air is the medium of both sound and color), while on the other hand,

425a   when there are multiple media for the same sensible, such as both air and water for color (since both are transparent), even a being having only one of them will perceive what passes through both; and sense organs are composed of only these two of the simple bodies, air and water (the eye of water, the ear of air, the organ of smell from both of them, while fire either belongs to none or is common to all, since nothing without heat is able to perceive, and earth either belongs to none or is especially involved in touch); then it would follow that there is no sense organ outside the ones of water and air, which several animals currently possess,

10   so that all the senses are possessed by the ones of these that are not incomplete or damaged (for even the mole evidently has eyes underneath its skin). Thus, if there is not some other kind of body, or some way of being acted upon that belongs to none of the bodies here, no sense would be left out.[1]

---

1   This complicated argument is easier to follow if one sees that Aristotle first establishes our possession of the full range for contact senses, and then shifts his attention to distance senses. Regarding the latter, he argues that, since both air and water serve as media for them, nature can achieve the full range of distance sensation through organs built around either air or water.

Neither, however, is there some special sense organ for the common things we perceive incidentally by each sense, such as motion, rest, figure, magnitude, number and unity. For we perceive all these by means of motion (for example, magnitude by means of motion, and therefore also figure, since figure is also a certain magnitude; and the resting thing by means of its not moving; and number by the negation of continuity) and by means of what is proper to each sense (for each perceives one). Thus it is clear that there cannot be a distinct sense for any of these, such as motion. Otherwise it will be like it is now when we perceive the sweet thing by sight: this is because we happen to have perception of both, by which we are aware of them at the same time when they occur together. But if this is not the case, then we will perceive it in no other way than incidentally: for example, in the case of the son of Cleon, we do not perceive that he is the son of Cleon, but that he is white, which the son of Cleon happens to be. Of the common things, however, we have a direct common perception, not a merely incidental one; there is not, therefore, a distinct sense for them, or else we would perceive them no differently than (as was just said) we see the son of Cleon.² But it is only incidentally that the senses perceive what is proper to one another, not insofar as they are themselves, but rather by being as one whenever perception occurs regarding the same thing, for example that bile is bitter and yellow; certainly it does not require some other sense to say

20

30

425b

---

2   The shifts in the argument here can be confusing, for two main reasons. (1) The first is that Aristotle is using "incidental" in two ways. In II.6, he distinguished proper sensibles, common sensibles and incidental sensibles. In the present passage he uses incidental first in a broad sense, to distinguish the way we perceive common sensibles from the way we perceive proper sensibles: The common sensibles are incidental to the proper sensibles in that they "come along with" them. But further on he points out that they are not entirely incidental, in that they are not connected by happenstance or perceived merely by inference or habitual connection, the way *strictly* incidental sensibles are. (2) The second reason for confusion is that he uses the example of the son of Cleon in two slightly different ways. The first time, the son of Cleon is the example of a strictly incidental sensible (in contrast to the tasteable and the visible, which are proper sensibles). The last time, he is the example of indirect perceiving in general (as we might perceive the sweet indirectly by sight, though each is proper to its own sense). Aristotle can make this shift because in the meantime he has stated emphatically that the common sensibles are *directly* implicated in the distinct senses. In short, common sensibles are like incidental sensibles in not being strictly connected to distinct senses, but unlike them in being directly implicit in what is perceived by the different distinct senses.

that they both are one. Thus one is also deceived, and believes that when something is yellow it is bile.

One might inquire why it is that we have several senses rather than just a single one. Or is it so that the accompanying and common things (like motion, magnitude and number) should not go unrecognized? If there were only sight, and it was of the white, we would more easily fail to notice them, and all things would even seem to be one same thing because of the way color and magnitude keep company with one another. As it is, since the common things also dwell in another kind of sensible, this makes it clear that each of them is something distinct.

III.2

Since, however, we perceive that we are seeing or hearing, one must perceive that one is seeing either by means of sight or by another sense. But in the latter case the same one will perceive the vision as well as the underlying color; thus either there will be two senses of the same thing or the same sense will perceive itself. Moreover, if there were another sense to perceive vision, either this will go on infinitely or eventually some sense will perceive itself, so that one ought to just posit this in the first instance. But this involves a perplexity: if perceiving by means of vision is seeing, and if what is seen is color or what has it, then if someone sees the thing that sees, the primary thing that sees will have color too. It is clear, then, that perceiving by means of sight is not one thing; for even when we do not see, we distinguish the darkness and light by means of sight, although not in the same way. Besides, the thing that sees is, indeed, colored, as it were. For each sense organ is receptive of the sensible without the material; hence, even once the sensible things have gone, the sensations and images are still in the sense organ.

The being-at-work of the sensible and of the sense is the same and is one, though their being is not the same—I mean, for example, the sound as it is at work and the hearing as it is at work. For it is possible for something that has hearing to not be hearing, and for something that has a sound to not be always sounding; but whenever something able to hear is working and something able to sound is sounding, then together they simultaneously become hearing at work and sound at work, these things of which someone might say that one is a hearing and the other a sounding. Indeed, if the motion and the action and the effect are in the thing acted upon, then both the sound and the hearing as being-at-work must be in the hearing power that exists as potential; for the being-at-work of that which is active and productive of motion comes about in the thing affected. (Hence it is not necessary for the thing that is the mover to be moved.) So then, the being-at-work of what is able to sound is sound or the act of sounding, while that of what is able to hear is the sense of hearing or the act of hearing; for hearing is twofold, and sound is twofold.[3] The account is the same in the cases of the other senses and sensibles. And just as the acting and the being acted upon are in the thing acted upon rather than in the thing acting, so also the being-at-work of the sensible and of the perceptive thing are both in the perceptive thing. But in some cases they are named (for example, sounding and hearing), while in others one is nameless—for the being-at-work of vision is called seeing, while that of color is nameless; and of what is capable of taste, it is tasting, while of flavor it is nameless.

10

And since the being-at-work of what can perceive and of what is perceptible is one, though their being is different, it is necessary for hearing and sound, meant in this way, to perish or to be preserved together, as well as flavor and taste and likewise the others; but when these things are meant as potential, it is not necessary. But those who first discoursed about nature did not speak well about this, since they believed that nothing was either white or black without sight, and that there was no flavor without taste. Indeed, they spoke correctly in one way and incorrectly in another: since perception and the perceptible are meant doubly, with respect to potential and with respect to being-at-work, what they said certainly accords well with the latter, but it does not with the former. They, however, spoke simply about things that are not meant simply.

20

Now if harmony is a sort of voice, and the voice and hearing are one in a certain way (while in another way not one or the same thing), and harmony is a *logos*, then the hearing has to also be a *logos*.[4] Because of this, each kind of excess, both the sharp and the flat, destroys the hearing, and excesses in flavor destroy taste, and in colors the excessively bright or obscure destroys vision, and in

30
426b

---

3   Sound is both (A) moving the air and (B) moving the ear so as to be heard; hearing is (C) possessing the power of hearing and also (D) the being-at-work of the power of hearing. B and D are the same thing, but viewed one way as having its active being from the action of the sounding thing and another way as having its active being from the potency of the sense and its organ.

4   Again, the primary meaning of *logos* here is "ratio", though it is also intended to evoke "form".

smell it is the strong smell, both sweet and bitter—just as though it is a certain *logos* of the sense. The pleasure also derives from this. For whenever things like the sharp and sweet and salty, from being pure and unmixed, are drawn toward a *logos*, then they are pleasant; and in general it is the mixed, rather than the sharp or flat, that is a harmony. For touch, it is the heated and the cooled; the sense is the *logos*, but the excessive either pains or destroys.

So then, each sense is of its sensible object, and resides in its sense organ insofar as it is a sense organ, and discriminates the differences within its sphere of perception (in the case of sight, white and black, or in the case of taste, sweet and bitter, and so on for the others). But since we distinguish the white and the sweet and each of the sensibles from each of the others, it is by means of something that we perceive that they differ. It is necessarily by means of a sense, since they are sensibles. By this it is clear that the flesh is not the ultimate organ of sense, for then it would have to be by touching it that what discriminates would discriminate. Nor, indeed, is it admissible that by means of the separate senses one discerns that the sweet is different from the white, but both of them must be manifest to some one thing—otherwise, it would be clear that they differ from one another even if I perceived one and you perceived the other. No, it must be a single thing that says it is different, for the sweet is different from the white. It is the same thing that says so; and as it says, so also it thinks and perceives.

Clearly then, separate things cannot be discriminated by separate senses—and not at separate times either, as is clear from the following. Just as the same thing says that the good and the bad are different, so also when it says the one differs it also says the other does, and this "when" is not incidental. I mean, for example, I am now saying that they differ, but not that they differ *now*; but it says so now and also that it is *now*, and therefore at the same time. Thus it is something indivisible that discriminates in an indivisible time.

But it is surely impossible for the same thing to be moved at the same time by contrary motions, insofar as the thing moved and the time are both indivisible. For, if it is sweet, it moves the sense and the thought this way, and the bitter the opposite way, and the white differently. Is it the case, then, that the thing that discriminates is one in number, indivisible, and inseparable in time, while at the same time separated in its being—so that it is somehow in one way, as divisible, that it perceives divided things, and in another way, as indivisible (i.e. divisible in its being, but

10

20

30

427a

indivisible in place, time and number)? Or is this not possible? For something that is the same and indivisible is potentially differentiated into contraries, but not differentiated in its being. It is differentiated through its coming to be at work, but is not able to be white and black at the same time; neither then can it be acted upon at the same time by the forms of these (if that is the sort of thing perception and thought are). Rather, it is like what some call a point: as this is either one or two, it is divisible in just this way.[5] So then, insofar as it is indivisible, that which discriminates is one and distinguishes things at the same time; but insofar as it is divisible, it is able to not be one, but simultaneously makes a double use of the same indicator. Insofar, then, as it makes use of a double boundary, it distinguishes two separate things and is as if divided; but insofar as it acts by means of one thing, it does so at one time.

10

So then, let the governing principle with respect to which we say that the animal is perceptive be delimited in this way.

III.3

Since the soul is demarcated mainly by two distinctive features—motion with respect to place and thinking and understanding—and since thinking and understanding seem like some kind of perceiving (for in both cases the soul discriminates something and recognizes the different beings), the ancients say that understanding and perceiving are the same thing. Thus Empedocles has said "wisdom increases for human beings according to what is present to them," and elsewhere, "hence different thoughts always present themselves to them;" and the verse of Homer, "for just so is the mind,"[6] means the same thing, for they all understood thinking to be bodily just like perceiving, and perceiving and thinking to be of like by like, just as we outlined in the initial discourses.[7] At the same time, they needed to account for being deceived the same way (for this is the more common lot for living things, and the soul passes the majority of its time in this condition). Hence it is necessary either, as some say, that all appearances are true, or that deception is contact with the unlike, since this is the opposite of recognizing like by like;

20

427b

---

5   A point cannot be divided, but can indicate either a place on a line or the two-sided boundary between two touching lines.

6   *Odyssey* 18.136

7   See Book I, especially chapters 2 and 5.

but then both deception and knowledge of opposites seem to be the same thing.

It is evident, then, that perceiving and understanding are not the same thing; for all animals have a share of the former, but few of the latter. But thinking, including thinking rightly and thinking not rightly (for thinking rightly is understanding and knowledge and true opinion, and thinking not rightly is the opposites of these)—this is not the same thing as perceiving either. For perception is always true, at least in regard to its proper objects, and belongs to all animals; but it is possible to think things through falsely as well, and that belongs to no animal that does not also have speech.

Imagination is a different thing from both perception and reflection. It does not come about without perception, and without it there is no supposing. But it is also evident that thought is not the same as supposing. For it is an experience that is up to us whenever we wish it (for it is possible to place things before one's eyes, just as is done by those who make images and arrange them in mnemonic schemas), whereas forming an opinion is not up to us, since it must be either false or true. Besides, whenever we have the opinion that something is terrible or frightening, we immediately experience the accompanying emotion (and likewise when it is something emboldening); but with imagination, we are disposed as if looking at a picture of terrible or emboldening things. Moreover, there are different kinds of supposing—knowledge and opinion and understanding and their opposites—whose differences belong to a different discourse.[8] As regards thinking, since it is something other than perceiving, and since both imagination and supposing seem to belong to it, it is only once we have demarcated imagination that we should speak of the other.

428a   So if imagination is that through which some image comes about for us (if one is to say something non-metaphorical about it), is it one of the potencies or states according to which we discriminate or are in a state of truth or falsehood, such as are perception, opinion, intellect and knowledge?

That it is not perception is clear from the following. While perception is either potential or at-work (for example, sight or seeing), something can nonetheless appear to us when neither of

10

20

---

8   Aristotle gives these topics a preliminary treatment in *Nicomachean Ethics* Book VI.

these obtains (for example, during sleep). Perception, moreover, is always present, while imagination is not. If, on the other hand, they are the same thing in their being-at-work, this would allow imagination to belong to all the animals, which seems not to be the case (for even if it is in the ant and the bee, it is not in the grub-worm).[9] Furthermore, perceptions are always true, while most imaginings turn out to be false. Besides, whenever we are at work perceiving accurately, we do not say about the perceived thing that it "appears" to us to be a human being, but only when we do not perceive quite clearly—for then there is both true and false appearance. And just as we said before, visual images occur even when the eyes are shut tight.

But surely it will not be one of the things that are always truthful, like knowledge or intellectual apprehension, since imagination is also false. It remains to be seen then whether it is opinion, for opinion also turns out both true and false. But in fact, conviction follows upon opinion, since it is not possible to form an opinion without being convinced of what seems to be the case; but conviction is not present in any of the beasts, whereas imagination is in many. Besides, while in every instance opinion presupposes conviction, conviction also presupposes having been persuaded, and persuasion presupposes *logos*; but while imagination is present in many beasts, *logos* is not. So it is clear, because of these things, that imagination would also not be opinion accompanied by perception or produced through perception, nor an interweaving of opinion and perception.[10] It is also clear because, if it were, then opinion will only be about that of which there is perception: in other words, if imagination is an interweaving of an opinion and perception of whiteness, not of an opinion of goodness and a perception of whiteness, then to imagine is to opine about just what is perceived non-incidentally. But there are false imaginings about which there is at the same time true judgment. For example, the sun appears a foot wide, but one is convinced that it is greater than the inhabited part of the earth. It follows that either one has tossed out the true opinion one had (while the thing has remained the same, and one has neither

10

20

30
428b

---

9   The texts of *On the Soul* that have come down to us (the earliest of which dates from the tenth century) deny imagination to all three, but ancient commentators seem to have been working with a text that reads as it does here. The ant and bee (to take the most obvious example) find their way back to the hill or hive as if they have a memory of place.

10   Cf. Plato, *Sophist* 264a.

forgotten nor been differently persuaded), or (if one still has it) it is necessary that the same opinion be both true and false. True opinion, however, becomes false only when the thing changes without one's noticing. Imagination, then, is not any one of these things, nor is it composed of them.

10   Since, however, when something is moved something else can be moved by it; and imagination seems to be some kind of motion, and to come about not without perception, but rather for things that perceive and of the things they perceive; and a motion occurs because of the being-at-work of perception (a motion that is necessarily similar to the perception)—then this motion is not possible without perception, nor does it belong to non-perceiving things, and the one who has it does and experiences many things in accord with it. It can also be either true or false, which comes about from the following. First, a perception of what is proper to its sense is true or has minimal falsehood. But it is secondarily

20   a perception of the thing to which these qualities belong, and here there is already room for error: one cannot mistake that it is white, but one can be mistaken whether it is this white thing or another. But in the third place, it is perception of the common sensibles that come along with these incidental sensibles to which the proper sensibles belong—I mean for example motion and magnitude (which accompany the sensible things), concerning which there is the greatest chance of being deceived in the course of perception. But the motion that comes about from the being-at-work of perception will differ as it takes its departure from these three kinds of sensibles. The first one is truthful while the perception is present, but the others may be false both when it is present and when it is absent, and especially whenever the thing perceived is far away.

30   So if nothing other than imagination has the characteristics
429a   spoken of, but it is what has been said, then imagination would be a motion coming about from perception in accord with its being-at-work. But since vision is perception in the highest degree, imagination (*phantasia*) has taken its name from light (*phaos*), because without light it is not possible to see.

And animals, because the images remain in them and are similar to the perceptions, perform many actions in accord with them—some, like the beasts, because they do not have intellect, others, like human beings, because their intellect is sometimes obscured either by illness or by sleep.

Let this much, then, be said about imagination, concerning what it is and on account of what.

III.4

Concerning the part of the soul by which the soul knows and   10
understands (whether it is separable or is not, indeed, separable in magnitude but only according to *logos*), one must investigate what distinctive difference it has, as well as how thinking ever comes about.

Now, if thinking is just like perceiving, then it would be either some kind of being acted upon by what is intelligible, or something like this but different.[11] It must, then, not be acted upon, but receptive of the form, with the potency to become like the form but not be the form itself; and, as what is perceptive is related to the perceptibles, so must the intellect bear a similar relationship to the intelligibles. Thus, since it thinks all things, it is necessary, just as Anaxagoras says, for it to be "unmixed" so that it may "master" them (that is, so that it may come to know them)—   20
for something foreign intruding into it impedes and obstructs it. Thus it is necessary for its nature to be nothing other than this: possibility.[12] Therefore what is called the intellect of the soul (and by intellect I mean that by which the soul thinks things through

---

11   Cf. II.5, 417b2-16, where Aristotle distinguishes two different senses of "being acted upon," and points out that we have no distinct names by which to differentiate them.

12   What Aristotle articulates in this sentence is somewhat paradoxical. A nature, as he explains in *Physics* II.1 (192b21-23), is "some cause and governing principle of moving and coming to rest in the thing to which it belongs primarily and in virtue of itself, not incidentally" (my translation). Thus to have a nature is to have a determinate measure that governs motion from within. The nutritive potency has its measure from the form of the being that it preserves, the kind and amount of material it needs to incorporate, and the life-span of that being; the perceptive potencies have their measures as means of the sensible qualities in their ranges; the locomotive potencies of various animals have their measures from the constraints within and against which they operate (including the kind of nutritive and perceptive life that animal has). Even imagination is limited by the particular sensations that originate it in a given being. Since intellect thinks all things, however, the only measure of its potency is the things that are, and the relations among them. Its very nature orients it such that it finds its measure outside itself; thus its nature is nothing other than the possibility to conform to that measure. (See *Metaphysics* V.12, 1020a4-6.) The word here translated "possibility" is "*dunaton*", the adjectival form of "*dunamis*" (potency/potential). In the medieval Latin tradition, the term for what Aristotle describes here is the "possible intellect."

and arrives at suppositions) is not actively one of the beings until it is thinking. Hence it is reasonable that it not be mixed with the body, for then it would take on some determinate quality, would be warm or cold, and there would be some organ for it as there is for the perceptive power—which there is not. And indeed, they speak well who say that the soul is a place of forms, except that it is not the whole soul but the intellective soul, and this is not the forms as being-fully-itself, but in potential.[13]

30   The sense in which the intellective power is not acted upon is not just like the case of the perceptive power. This is clear with regard to the sense organs and perception. Perception is rendered

429b   unable to perceive by a powerful sensible—for example, to perceive sound amid loud sounds, or to see or smell amid intense colors or odors. Intellect, on the other hand, when it thinks something powerfully intelligible, is not less able to think lesser things, but even more able; for the perceptive power does not exist without body, but intellect is separate. Once it has come to be each of the intelligibles, as when one is said to be an active knower (which is the case when one is able to be at work on one's own), even then it is in a certain way the intelligibles in potential, though of course not like the way it was before it learned or discovered them; for now it is able to think itself.

10   Since a magnitude is something different from the being of magnitude, and water from the being of water (and so also for many other things, but not for all, since for some it is the same thing), it is either by means of something different or by the same thing disposed in a different way that one discriminates flesh and

---

13   Aristotle may have in mind the notion of recollection as presented in some of Plato's dialogues, according to which the intelligible forms of things are somehow already "in" the soul unconsciously, as if they were seen and forgotten until the intellect rediscovers them (thereby becoming fully what it already is according to a pre-determined potential). It is also illuminating to contrast Aristotle with Kant, for whom the understanding has an inherent structure that it gradually discovers in the course of exercising itself. In both the Kantian view and the idea of recollection, the power of intellect is commingled with the power of memory: for it is our memory (including the memory of the thoughts we have had) that takes on a structure as the result of our thinking (and all our other experiences). Aristotle is trying to say what the power of thought itself is, considered in separation from other powers like memory (which is a certain mode of imagination; cf. On Memory and Recollection 450a11-14). Unlike memory and imagination, the power of thought remains unaltered by experience, although the alterations of memory and imagination through experience give it more occasions for insight.

the being of flesh. For there is no flesh without material, but, like the snub-nosed, it is a this in a that.[14] Now, it is by means of the perceptive power that one discriminates the hot and the cold and the things of which flesh is a certain *logos*; but the being of flesh is discriminated by something else, either separate or disposed the way a line that has been bent is toward itself when it is straightened out.[15] Or again, in the case of things that exist by way of abstraction, the straight is like the snub, since it presupposes continuous magnitude; but the being of what it is (if the straight and the being of the straight are different) is something else (say, twoness). Therefore one discriminates it either by something different or by the same thing differently disposed. And in general, therefore, the way things are separable from their material is also the way it is with what concerns the intellect.

    One might be perplexed, though: if the intellect is simple and not acted upon and has nothing in common with anything, as Anaxagoras says, how will it think, if thinking is being acted upon in some way? For it seems that it is only insofar as there is something in common that one thing acts and another is acted upon. One might further wonder whether even the intellect itself is intelligible. For then, either there will be intellect in the other things (if it is not intelligible owing to something else, but the intelligible is some one thing in kind), or it will have something mixed with it, which makes it knowable itself just like the other things are. Or else it is the case (in accord with the way of being acted upon by something common that was distinguished earlier[16]) that the intellect is somehow the intelligibles in potential, but not by way of being-fully-itself until it thinks them. It must be just like when

20

30

430a

---

14   That is, a concave shape in a nose. The snub is Aristotle's favorite example of something in which the material and the form are inseparably implied.

15   Ronald Polansky (*Aristotle's De Anima*, pp.445-451) helpfully suggests that this analogy may apply, in different ways, both to perception and to intellect. Perception is primarily (i.e. when "straight") of proper sensibles (like hot and cold), but in a more indirect ("bent") way of incidental sensibles, like the magnitude or even the distinct being of a thing (as when we incidentally perceive a human being). Intellect, on the other hand, is primarily of the distinct being of things, but also distinguishes individual instances of them from one another (for example, when we have to reflect on the indicators that allow us to discern which of two twins is which). Since the "common sense faculty" is, in either case, the mediating power, the image of the bent line may also recall Aristotle's comparison of it to a point serving as a uniting boundary (III.2, 427a10).

16   417b2-16.

a writing tablet has nothing present on it that has become fully itself by being written out; this very thing occurs in the case of the intellect.[17] And it is itself intelligible the same way the intelligibles are. For in the case of things that are without material, the thing thinking and the thing thought are the same—for contemplative knowledge and what is thus known are the same thing. (The cause of its not being always thinking must be considered.) And in the things that have material, what is intelligible is present in each case only as potentially intelligible. Thus *intellect* will not be present in these (since intellect is a potency to be such things *without* the material), but what is intelligible will be present in *it*.

III.5

10   Since, however, in every nature there is something that is material for each kind (which is all those things in potential), while there is something else causal and productive, by which they are all produced (for example, the way art is in relation to its material), these differences must necessarily also be present in the soul. And indeed there is one sort of intellect that is such by becoming all things, and another by producing all things, as a kind of active disposition like light; for, in some way, light makes the colors that exist in potential be colors at work.[18] And this latter intellect is separate and unmixed and not acted upon, since it has being-at-work as its substantial being (for that which acts is always of a higher stature than that which is acted upon, and so too the

20   governing principle than the material). Knowledge at work is the same thing as the thing it knows; knowledge as potential is prior in time in the particular knower, but viewed more generally it is not even prior in time—for it is not at one time thinking and at

---

17   Again, it is necessary to sharply distinguish intellect from memory to avoid confusing what Aristotle says here with the later use of this image of the "blank slate" associated with John Locke's empiricism. (Significantly, the image Locke uses in *An Essay Concerning Human Understanding* is "white paper" [II.I.2].) Aristotle is not saying that the blank mind is progressively filled up with the impressions that are written on it. Rather, like a wax tablet that is written on and then smoothed out again to receive new writing, the nature of the intellect is to be always receptive, able to take on the form of whatever intelligible thing is present to it. Just as writing is not fully itself when we merely imagine letters, but only when it becomes a means of communicating by being written down, so the intelligible, to be fully what it is as intelligible, must be thought by what is receptive to it (except perhaps in the case of divine intellect, which is always fully at work; cf. *Metaphysics* XII.7).

18   Cf.418b19-20

another not thinking. Only when separated is this just what it is, and this alone is undying and eternal.[19] But we do not remember, because this is not acted upon, while the intellect that is acted upon is perishable, and without it nothing thinks.

III.6

Thinking that is of indivisible things is among those things concerning which there is no falsehood. In those where there is both falsehood and truth, on the other hand, there is already some composition of thoughts as a unity; just as Empedocles said that "then foreheads aplenty bloomed forth without necks" and were 30 then brought together by Love, so also these separate things are brought together by thought, such as the incommensurable and the diagonal of the square. And when it is of past or future things, 430b it brings time into its thinking and conjoins it. When there is falsehood, it is always in a composition, for when one says that the white thing is not white, one has conjoined the not-white to it. (It is also possible to say all things in terms of division.) It is certainly not only true or false that Cleon is white, but also that he was or will be. That which produces unity in each case is the intellect.

But since something is undivided in two ways (i.e. either without potential to be divided or without actively being divided), nothing prevents one from thinking indivisibly whenever one thinks of length (for it is not actively divided)—nor from doing so in an undivided time, since time is divisible and indivisible similarly to length. Nor is it possible to say that one thinks 10 separately of each half, since before it gets divided, the half does not exist, except in potential. But in thinking each of the halves separately one also simultaneously divides the time (and then it is

---

19   Cf. Plato, *Republic* X, 611b-612a. The obscurity of this chapter has generated controversy through the ages. On the one hand, by saying that it is "in the soul," Aristotle suggests that what he is calling "productive intellect" is part of human nature. On the other hand, by characterizing it as always at work and as producing all things, he puts us in mind of his description of divine intellect in *Metaphysics* XII.7. The claim that "this alone is undying and eternal" seems to make the question of the immortality of the human soul hinge on the question whether this intellect is properly part of us or not. Thus in the thirteenth century, the accurate interpretation of this chapter became a raging question bearing on the ultimate compatibility of Aristotle and Christian belief, with Thomas Aquinas arguing that "agent intellect" belonged to human nature, in opposition to the tradition stemming from the Aristotelian commentaries of the Muslim philosopher Averroes.

as if it were a length). And if one thinks of it as composed of both, one also does so in a time that embraces both.

As for that which is indivisible not according to quantity but rather in form, one thinks it in an indivisible time and with something indivisible in the soul. But that by which one thinks and the time in which one thinks are divisible incidentally, not insofar as the things it thinks are what they are, but insofar as they are divisible.[20] For there is something indivisible in these things (though perhaps not separable) which makes the time be one and the length be one—and this is in everything continuous, both in time and in length.

A point, however, and every divider and what is indivisible in this way, manifests itself in the way privation does; and it is a similar story in the case of other things, such as how one recognizes what is bad or what is black, since in some way one recognizes them by means of their opposites. But that which recognizes them has to be them in potential and they have to be one in it. (But if there is something with no opposite among the causes, it knows itself and exists as being-at-work and is separate.)

An assertion says something about something (like an affirmation), and every assertion is either true or false. But it is not so for every act of intellect: that which thinks what something is with respect to the very being of what it is does not think something about something; and it is true.[21] But just as the seeing of what is proper to sight is true, while whether the white thing is a man or not is not always true, so too does it hold for as many things as are without material.

---

20   The text here reads "indivisible" (*a-diaireta*), and there is much disagreement over how to make sense of it. On the assumption that a scribal error may be responsible for an added "*a*", I have interpreted the passage to mean the following. When we think of things that (like a circle) have some formal unity but also have divisible magnitude, our thinking can be divided and apportioned out to parts of what we all along still recognize as a unity. But this apportionment is possible because of the fact that the thing has magnitude, not because of the formal principle that makes it the unified thing it is. In this way the paragraph nicely complements the preceding one: The first paragraph explains that what has continual magnitude is nonetheless grasped as a whole, and this one explains that what has wholeness, if it is a magnitude, can be thought of as parts while one still holds in mind the thought of its wholeness.

21   Compare *Metaphysics* IX.10, 1051b18-1052a12.

III.7

Knowledge at work is the same thing as the thing it knows. 431a
Knowledge as potential is prior in time in the particular knower,
but viewed more generally it is not even prior in time; for all things
that come into being arise from something existing as fully itself.
It is clear that the perceptible thing causes the power of perception
to pass from existing as a potency to being at work, since the
perceptive power is neither acted upon nor altered. Hence this
is some other form of motion. For motion turned out to be the
being-at-work of something incomplete;[22] but the being-at-work
simply of what is already completed is different.

Now perceiving is similar to simple asserting and thinking;
but whenever one perceives a pleasant or painful thing, one 10
pursues or avoids it, as though affirming or denying. And being
pleased or being pained is the being-at-work of the perceptual
mean in relation to the good or bad insofar as the things are such.
In their being-at-work, avoidance and desire are the same thing;
and the desiring part and avoiding part do not differ either from
one another or from the perceptive part, although their being is
different.

But for the soul that thinks things through, images take the
place of perceptibles; and whenever they are good or bad, it affirms
or denies, avoids or pursues. This soul, therefore, never thinks
without an image. And just as the air makes the eyeball be such-
and-such a way, and then this does the same to something else, so
it also happens the same way in the hearing; but the thing they end
up at is one, and is a single mean, though its being is multiple. What 20
it is by which it determines what the difference between sweet and
hot is has already been said earlier,[23] but it should also be spoken
of now. It is some one thing, but in such a way as a boundary is.
And these things being united by way of analogy as well as by way
of something that is one in number, it stands toward each of them

---

22 *Physics* III.1

23 I.e. what comes to be called the *sensus communis* or common faculty of
sense, discussed earlier in III.2, 426b12ff.

as they stand toward one another.[24] For what difference is there between puzzling over how it distinguishes things that are not the same in kind and how it distinguishes opposite things like white and black? So let A (white) be to B (black) as C is to D, so that by alternation A:C::B:D. So if C and D belonged to one thing, they will have the same relation as A and B: while they are the same thing and one, their being is not the same thing (and moreover this is so in a similar way). But it is the same argument [or ratio: *logos*] even if A were sweet and B were white.

431b   So then it is in the images that the intellective power thinks the forms. And just as what is to be pursued or avoided is determined by it in the case of perceptibles, so also (even when it is removed from sensing) whenever it is engaged with images it is moved. For example, perceiving that the beacon is a fire, it recognizes by means of the common sense (because it sees it moving) that it is an enemy; but sometimes it reckons by means of the images and thoughts in the soul just as if it were seeing, and deliberates about the things to come on the basis of things present. And whenever it says that something is pleasant or painful, as in the case of perception so also in this case (and in action in general),

---

24   The relationships Aristotle is describing very tersely here are complicated. The hot and sweet are alike but different, and these relationships are founded in the nature of things. Hot and sweet can be united by belonging to something one in number (a freshly baked cookie), and this relationship of belonging together is reproduced in their togetherness in the common sense faculty. They are also different in that they are perceptibles belonging to different senses; and as they differ from one another, the common sense faculty (like a boundary point) distinguishes each from the vantage point of the other. But because it simultaneously relates them to the thing to which they belong and distinguishes them both from it, this dual recognition can serve as the basis for recognizing them as united in an analogy: they are both "sensible qualities" and, as such, both different from the thing of which they are qualities, but different in the same way.

This whole set of interrelated relationships illustrates the movement from the combining and distinguishing capacity of sensation to the combining and distinguishing capacity of thought. While sensation can unite things that are in some way continuous (two parts of a line, or two different adjacent colors) by the distinction that serves as a boundary between them, thought can rise to the level of analogy and proportion, that is, of recognizing that the likeness-and-difference between two things is the same in form as the likeness-and-difference between two other things.

As we think through the relationships between the various images, the sameness of relation becomes present to our intellect. This sameness is not itself an image, but is present in the images; thus it illustrates the relationship between imagination and intellect that Aristotle obscurely describes at the end of II.8. (Cf. Plato, *Republic* VI, 509d-e.)

it avoids or pursues. And even in what does not concern action, the true and the false are the same in kind with the good and bad; but they differ in that the former are simply so, and the latter are so for something or someone. As for the things said to exist in abstraction, it thinks them just as if it were thinking the snub: insofar as it is snub, it is not thought separately; insofar as it is concave, if someone were at work thinking it, they would think it without the flesh in which the concavity resides. Thus, though they are not separated, it thinks mathematical things as separated whenever it is thinking them.

    Considered as a whole, then, intellect in its being-at-work is the things it thinks. Whether or not it is possible for it to think something among separated things while itself not being separate from a magnitude remains to be considered later.

III.8

    Now, drawing together the things that have been said about soul, let us state again that the soul is somehow all the beings. The beings are either perceptible or intelligible; and while knowledge is in some way the knowable things, perception is the perceptible things. In what way this is so must be investigated.

    With a view to the things they are concerned with, knowledge and perception are divided into faculties existing as potency in relation to potential objects, and faculties fully themselves in relation to objects fully themselves. The parts of soul capable of perceiving and knowing are, in potential, these knowable and perceptible things. But they must either be the things themselves or the forms. To be sure, they are not the things themselves: the stone is not in the soul, but rather the form. Thus the soul is just like the hand; for the hand is a tool of tools, and intellect is a form of forms, and perception a form of perceptibles.[25]

---

25   Aristotle has said earlier (412b28) that the being-fully-itself of a tool such as an axe is its doing the work it is made for (i.e. chopping). The fact that human beings produce hand tools that lie around until used results in a curious state of affairs: the hand becomes, as it were, the instrument of all these tools that enables them to be fully themselves. So also, when we are surrounded by potentially knowable things, or (more relevantly to this chapter) when we have formed images in which knowable things are enabled to lie embedded and dormant in our memories, the intellect exists as a pure principle of form, enabling the intelligible forms latent in them to become fully what they potentially are. Perception is related the same way to perceptible forms in the things around us.

But since there is no thing that exists as separate apart from the perceptible magnitudes (or so it seems), it is in the perceptible forms that one finds the intelligible things—both the things said to exist in abstraction and any active dispositions and passive attributes of the perceptible things. On account of this, without perceiving one would not be able to learn or comprehend anything; and whenever one contemplates, it is necessary to contemplate some image at the same time (for images are like perceptions, except without material). Imagination, however, is different from affirmation and denial, since the true or false is an interweaving of thoughts. But in what respect will the primary thoughts differ from being images? These are not images, but are not present without images either.

III.9

Since the soul of animals is demarcated by two potencies (the power of distinguishing, which is the work of thinking and perception, and in addition the power of moving with regard to change of place), let the foregoing delineations regarding perception and intellect be sufficient. Regarding what it is in the soul that is responsible for motion, one must examine whether it is some one part of soul (separate either in magnitude or in *logos*), or the whole soul; and if some part, then whether it is to be called something peculiar to itself apart from the usual parts already spoken of, or whether it is some one of them.

But right away there is a perplexity involved in how one ought to say there are parts of soul and how many. For in some way they seem unlimited, and not merely the ones some distinguish, calling them the reasoning and spirited and appetitive, or as others say, the part having reason and the irrational part.[26] For according to the differences by which these are separated, there also appear to be other parts with a greater divergence than these, concerning which we have just now spoken: the nutritive, which is present both in the plants and in all the animals, and the perceptive, which one could easily place as neither irrational nor having reason. Moreover the imaginative, which differs from the rest in its being, but in some way is the same as some of them or different from

10

20

30

432b

---

26   The first division into three parts occurs most prominently in Book IV of Plato's *Republic* (though Socrates leaves open the possibility that there are other parts [443d]). Plato also uses the second division, as does Aristotle in contexts where he is being less precise for practical purposes (e.g. *Nicomachean Ethics* 1102a26-28).

them, involves much perplexity if someone will posit separated parts of the soul. Beyond these there is the desiring, which would seem both in *logos* and in potency to be different from the rest. But it is strange to scatter this about: for wish arises in the reasoning part, and appetite and spiritedness in the non-rational part; so if the soul is threefold, there will be desire in each part.

Concerning the particular point at which our discourse has now arrived: What is it that moves the animal with respect to place? Motion with respect to growth and withering, which belongs to all living things, would seem to be set in motion by the generative and nutritive capacity belonging to them all. Investigations concerning breathing in and out, and sleep and waking, must be taken up later, since these involve much perplexity.[27] What is to be investigated now, concerning motion with respect to place, is what it is that moves the animal with respect to progressive motion.

That it is not the nutritive potency is quite clear, since movement is always for the sake of something, and is accompanied by either imagination or desire. For nothing is moved that is not desiring or fleeing, except by force. Moreover, if the plants were also capable of moving, they would have some part serving as an organ for this kind of motion.

Nor, likewise, is it the perceptive, since there are many animals that have perception but are stationary and unable to move to the end of their days. If, therefore, nature neither does anything in vain nor leaves out any of the necessary things, except in things that are maimed or incomplete, while animals such as these are complete and not maimed (which is indicated by the fact that they are generative and have a peak of maturity and a decline), then they would have had the parts that are organs of progression.

Neither, however, is it the noetic (i.e. what is called intellect) that is the mover: the contemplative intellect does not contemplate anything to be done nor say anything about what is to be avoided or pursued, while movement is always of avoiding or pursuing something. And even if it does contemplate something of this sort, it still does not command avoidance or pursuit. One often, for example, thinks of something fearsome or pleasant, but it does not tell one to fear, but rather the heart is set in motion (or, in the case of the pleasant, some other part). Besides, it also happens that, when intellect orders and thought says to pursue or avoid

10

20

30

433a

---

27   Aristotle has a number of short treatises devoted to such topics, e.g. *On Respiration* and *On Sleep and Waking*.

something, one is not moved but acts according to appetite, as in those lacking self-command. And generally we see that one who has the medical art might not heal, since it is something else that determines our acting according to knowledge, but not the knowledge itself. Neither, however, is desire determinative of this kind of motion: those who have self-command, though they desire and crave, yet do not do the things for which they have desire, but follow the intellect.

III.10

These two, at least, are apparently causes of movement: either desire or intellect (if one would classify imagination as a kind of thinking). In many cases humans follow their imaginations in spite of their knowledge; and in the other animals there is no thought or reasoning, but there is imagination. Both these, then, are productive of motion with respect to place: intellect and desire—that is, intellect which reasons for the sake of something and is practical, which differs from the contemplative in its end. All desire is for the sake of something; that which is the object of desire is the starting point of practical intellect, and the latter's conclusion is the starting point of action. Thus, quite reasonably, these two are apparent as movers—desire and practical thinking—since what is desired causes movement, and, through this, thinking causes movement because its starting point is what is desired. And whenever imagination causes movement, it does not do so without desire.

Some one thing, then, is the mover: that which is desired. For if two were the movers—intellect and desire—then they would be movers according to some shared form. As it is, however, intellect is manifestly not a mover without desire; for wish is desire, and whenever one moves according to reasoning, one moves according to wish as well. But desire can cause motion in spite of reasoning, for appetite is a kind of desire. All intellectual apprehension is correct, while desire and imagination are both correct and not correct. Hence what causes motion is always what is desired, but this is either the good or the apparent good. Not every good, however, but the practical good (and a practical good is one that admits of being otherwise).

So then it is clear that such a potency of the soul, what is being called desire, causes motion. For those, then, who distinguish the parts of the soul, if they distinguish and divide them according to the potencies, the parts turn out to be many: nutritive, perceptive, intellective, deliberative, and desiderative (for these differ more from one another than the appetitive from the spirited). The desires, however, also come to be opposed to one another, which occurs whenever reason and the appetites are opposed; and this comes about in beings that have perception of time, since intellect bids us resist on account of the consequences, while appetite is on account of the immediate (for the immediate appears pleasant, and simply pleasant, and simply good, on account of not seeing the consequences). In form, the mover would be one: the desiderative as desiderative. But the first of all is what is desired, since, while not itself being moved, this causes motion by being thought or imagined. In number, then, the movers are many.

10

Movement involves three things: one is what causes motion, second is that by which it causes motion, and then third is that which is moved. But that which causes motion is twofold: one kind is the unmoved, and the other is what causes motion while being also moved. So then the unmoved is the good to be attained by action, while what causes motion and is moved is the desiderative (for that which desires is moved insofar as it desires, and desire is some kind of motion or being-at-work). What is moved is the animal; and as for the instrument by means of which desire causes motion, this now is something bodily (and hence we must contemplate these matters in the works common to body and soul together).[28] To speak here by way of summary: what causes motion instrumentally is where a beginning and an end are in the same place, such as a joint; for here the concave and convex are the ending and beginning (being different in *logos* but inseparable in magnitude), such that the one is at rest and the other is in motion (for all things are moved by way of pushing and pulling). Thus, just as in the case of a circle, it is necessary for something to remain fixed, and for the motion to start from there.

20

In general, then, as has been said, in the way in which the animal is desiderative, in just such a way is it able to move itself; and it is not desiderative without imagination. All imagination is either sensory or involves reasoning. The other animals thus have a share in this as well.

30

---

28 Aristotle treats such questions in more detail in *Parts of Animals*, *Movement of Animals*, and *Progression of Animals*, but distills some of the principal insights of those discussions in the sentences that follow here.

III.11

434a
But one ought to inquire also about the imperfect animals: what is it that causes motion in animals whose only sense is that of touch, and is it possible for imagination (and also appetite) to belong to them or not? Evidently there is pain and pleasure in them. But if these are present, appetite necessarily is too. But how would imagination exist in them? Or is it that, just as they are in motion indeterminately, so also these exist in them, but are in them indeterminately?

10
Now sensory imagination, as has been said, is present even in the unreasoning animals, while deliberative imagination is present in the reasoning ones. For the question whether one will do this or that is already a work of reasoning, and it always requires a single measure; for one pursues what is better, so that out of many images it is able to produce a single one. On account of this, it does not seem the case that imagination has opinion, because it is not imagination that has the opinion that results from the syllogism, but the latter has the former.[29] Hence desire does not have the deliberative capacity, but sometimes it conquers and pushes aside deliberative wish, and at other times the reverse happens, as in a game of balls; or desire will so act on desire, when there is lack of self-command. By nature, however, it is the higher one that is more the governing principle and causes motion. Thus there are three ways of being moved.[30]

---

29   Cf. III.3, 428a20-24. The Greek sentence here does not have the word "imagination" (*phantasia*), and the reference is quite unclear. Some interpreters take Aristotle to be referring to unreasoning animals as not having *opinion*. I believe Aristotle wants to account for the fact that our imagination includes images that are charged with our desires. This is not because imagination itself is, as such, suffused with desire, but rather because the deliberative process (even, let us say, if it occurs subconsciously) identifies something as desirable, and this determination then gets embedded in the image that is in us. Thus it is deliberate opinion that takes hold of imagination as a receptacle for desire. Human beings are active interpreters of what appears good to them, because they have the deliberative capacity that weighs relative goods and is perfected in practical wisdom (the condition described further on as "by nature"). In our search for the good, we constantly reconfigure the relative desirability associated with the images in our imaginations.

30   Again, the specific reference is unclear. Given the lines along which the thought has been developing, it seems most reasonable to identify the "three ways" as distinguished by the efficacy of the deliberative desire that ought to be ruling. Sometimes it rules, sometimes it is defeated, and sometimes it leaves the field open to the conflict of immediate desires.

The faculty of knowledge does not move something, but remains stationary. But since one supposition or *logos* is general and the other concerns the particular (for the former says it is necessary to do a certain sort of thing, while the latter says that this here and now is that sort of thing and I am that sort of person), it is the latter opinion that immediately causes motion, not the general one. Or it is both, but the one is at rest and the other is not.   20

III.12

It is necessary for every thing whatsoever that is going to live to have nutritive soul, and it has soul from its generation until its destruction. For a thing that is generated necessarily has growth, maturity and decline; and these are impossible without nourishment. Thus nutritive potency is necessarily present in all things that grow and decline. Perception, on the other hand, is not necessarily present in all living things, since those whose body is simple cannot have touch (without which nothing can be an animal), and neither can things that are not receptive of forms   30
without material.

But an animal must necessarily have perception, if nature produces nothing in vain. For all things that exist by nature exist for the sake of something, or will be attributes of what is for the sake of something. So every mobile body, if it lacked perception, would perish and not arrive at its fulfillment, which is the work of   434b
nature. How will it nourish itself? Now for stationary beings, on the one hand, this is present where they have grown. On the other hand, it is not possible for a body to have soul and discriminating intellect but not have perception, if it is not stationary and is generated (and indeed even if it is not generated). For why will this be the case? It must be better either for the soul or for the body. But in fact it is neither: the former will not think better, nor will the latter better exist on account of that. Thus no body that moves itself has soul without perception.

Now then, if it has perception, its body is necessarily either simple or mixed. It cannot, however, be simple, for then it will not   10
have touch—and having this is a necessity, which is clear from the following. Since the animal is an ensouled body, and every body is tangible, and a tangible thing is what is perceptible by touch, the body of the animal must also have the sense of touch if it is going to preserve itself. For the rest of the senses perceive through other things (i.e. smell, sight and hearing); but if something is touched, if it does not have perception, it will not be able to avoid

some things and take hold of others. But in that case it will be impossible for the animal to preserve itself. Hence taste is also a kind of touch, since it is of nourishment, and the nourishment is a tangible body. Sound and color and smell do not nourish, nor do they produce either growth or decay. Thus taste must also be some kind of touch, since it is perception of the tangible and nourishing. These are certainly necessary to the animal, so it is obvious that there cannot be an animal without touch.

The other senses are for the sake of living well, and they necessarily pertain already not just to any animal whatsoever, but to certain kinds. A mobile animal, if it is going to preserve itself, must perceive not only when it is touched, but also from afar. This would be the case if it were able to perceive through a medium, from the medium being acted upon and moved by what is perceptible and the animal in turn by it. For it is just like that which causes motion with respect to place, which produces change up to a certain point: that which pushes another thing makes the latter push as well; the movement occurs through an intermediary; the first mover pushes without being pushed, while what is last is only pushed and does not push; and the intermediaries are many. So it is in the case of alteration as well, except that it alters something that remains in the same place, like when one presses into wax and it is moved only so far as one has pressed. A stone would not be moved at all, but water would for some distance, while air is moved a great deal and acts and is acted upon, if it remains stable and unified. Hence, as regards reflection, it is better to say, not that the sight that goes forth is reflected back, but that the air is acted upon by the shape and color as long as it remains unified. On a smooth surface it is unified, and hence the surface moves the sight, just as if the seal in the wax passed all the way to the other end.

III.13

It is evident that the body of an animal cannot be simple—I mean, for example, fiery or airy. For without touch it will not admit of having any other sense, given that (as has been said) ensouled body as a whole is capable of touch. The other sense organs could come to be from elements aside from earth; but they all produce perception by means of perceiving through something else and through a medium, whereas touch involves touching things (hence the very name it bears). To be sure, the other sense organs also perceive by touch, but on account of something other than themselves, while this sense alone seems to perceive on account of itself. Thus, as for those sorts of elements, no one of them could be the body of an animal. Nor is it composed just of earth. For touch exists as a mean of all the tangible qualities, and its sense organ is receptive not just of whatever differences of earth there are, but also of heat and cold and all the other tangibles. And this is why we do not perceive by means of bones or hairs or other such parts, because they are earthy. It is also because of this that the plants do not have a single sense, because they are earthy; but without touch, no other sense can be present, while the sense organ of touch is made neither all of earth nor of any single one of the other elements.

20

435b

Now it is evident that animals deprived of this single sense will necessarily die. For without this it is not possible for something to be an animal, nor does any sense other than this necessarily belong to something that is an animal. For this reason, an animal is not destroyed by the excesses of the other sensibles (such as color, sound or smell), but only its sense organs are (except perhaps incidentally, for example if a thrust or blow arises in company with the sound, or when by visible things or a smell other things are set in motion that destroy by means of touch). Even flavor is destructive only insofar as something tangible happens to come along with it. The excess of tangibles, however, such as hot or cold or hard things, does away with an animal; for the excess of every sensible does away with the sense organ, so that the tangible thus acts upon touch, but this is coextensive with being alive (since it has been shown that without touch it is impossible to be an animal). Hence the excess of the tangibles destroys not only the sense organ, but the very animal, because it is only this that it is necessary for animals to have.

10

The animal has the other senses, as was said, not for the sake of being, but for the sake of well-being. It has vision, for example, so that it can see, since it lives in air or water, or generally in the transparent; and it has taste on account of the pleasant and painful, so that it may perceive this in its nutriment and desire it and move itself; while it has hearing so that something may be signified to it, and a tongue so that it may signify something to another.

20

GLOSSARY

Affections (*pathe*). The experiences or qualitative changes that something undergoes, usually as a result of being acted upon by something else. Aristotle speaks of "affections of soul" in Book I, initially emphasizing emotions. As it turns out, however, *On the Soul* is not about such affections, but rather about soul's **potencies** and their **being-at-work**. In II.5, Aristotle makes clear that a potency's being set to work by its proper object is not so much an affection or being acted upon by something foreign or qualitatively different; rather, it is a case of the potency's being brought into **being-fully-itself**.

Attributes (*ta sumbebeka*). See **Incidental**

Being-at-work (*energeia*). As Aristotle explains in *Metaphysics* IX.6, being-at-work cannot be defined so much as understood as the correlate to **Potential/Potency** (*dunamis*). The bronze that is the potential **material** for a statue can be made by the sculptor to be at work doing what statues do (representing something, staying upright, orienting a space around itself, commanding attention and inspiring). The potency of hearing can be brought into being-at-work by a sound that meets it. One distinctive feature that differentiates something truly meriting the name "being-at-work" from something more properly called a motion is that the being-at-work is complete at every moment. The statue continues to represent as long as it continues to be a statue, and hearing hears at the same time as it has heard; but motion from place to place or alteration from one color to another happens by parts and stages. (See *On the Soul* III.7, 431a1-8.) Being alive is not a kind of motion, but a kind of being-at-work more adequately characterized as a thing's **being-fully-itself**.

Being-fully-itself (*entelecheia*). Aristotle coins this word by taking "*endelecheia*" (persistence or continuity) and sticking "*telos*" (fulfillment, end, final **cause**) into the middle of it. It might most literally be translated "persisting in completeness" and denotes a thing's active self-sustaining as what it is. We sometimes speak of being "truly alive" when we are exercising our **potencies** to the utmost; but since we can rarely if ever do this (for in fact it is less possible the more complex an array of potencies a living being has), the more basic, modest and stable sense in which we and other living beings are alive is by actively maintaining those potencies in their potential for operating. This is what Aristotle describes as the "first" being-fully-itself of a living thing, which is what soul is.

Being-what-it-is (*to ti en einai*). When Aristotle speaks of "the being" of something, he means not the "fact" that it is present in the world, but refers rather to that which makes it what it is and is intelligible as its **Distinct Being**. To express this, he uses "*to einai*" ("the to be") with the dative case of the thing (thus "*to sarki einai*" is literally "the to be for flesh", and means "the being of flesh" or "what it is to be flesh"). The expression "*to ti en einai*" (which originates with Aristotle) translates literally as "the to be what it was." The central part of the expression, "*ti en*" or "what it was" suggests the insight into a thing's being that results from philosophical inquiry. Socrates always asked of things like justice or virtue, "What is it?" (*Ti esti*). "*En*" is the past tense of "*esti*" and has a progressive or continuous aspect. Hesiod uses it in *Works and Days* when he tells his brother that, although he thought there was only one kind of Strife, it turns out there have been two kinds all along. So "*ti en*" means something like "what it turns out the thing was all the time one was seeking to uncover what it is." Thus when Aristotle says soul is "the being-what-it-is of a certain kind of [natural] body" (II.1, 412b11), this is shorthand for saying that, if you understand what a certain kind of living being is by examining its **form** and organization, and the complex of life-activities these make possible, soul will be what it is to *be* and to *go on being* that being you have come to understand—and that this is true for any kind of living being.

Categories (*kategoriai*). The different ways of being, or the most inclusive classes (*gene*) into which distinct phenomena are articulated. Aristotle discusses them extensively in *Categories* and briefly in *Metaphysics* V.7. The principal category is **Substantial Being**; the other ways of being all ultimately belong to and depend upon the being of substantial beings. The secondary categories are: Quantity, Quality, Relation, Acting, Being Acted Upon, Being at a Time, Being in a Place, Being in a Position, and Having a Disposition (although the last two are not included in the list in the *Metaphysics*).

Cause (*aitia*). A **governing principle** responsible for a thing's being what it is and as it is. In *Physics* II.3, Aristotle distinguishes four ways of being a cause of something: as its **form**, as its **material**, as an origin of motion, and as the completion or end (*telos*) or "that for the sake of which" it is as it is.

Contemplation (*theoria*); **contemplate** (*theorein*). To contemplate is to be absorbed in focused attentiveness to something. In a broad sense, it can refer to attention given to anything. In a more distinctive sense, it refers to reflective attention to the unchanging aspect of beings in the world, which typically means attention to our own images of those beings (see "**Imagination**" and part 3 of the Introduction) in the attempt to render our **intellect** receptive to what is intelligible in those beings. Thus the contemplative (*theoretike*) sciences are those that concern the unchanging intelligible **governing principles** of beings (namely, **first philosophy**, natural philosophy, and mathematics).

Distinct Being (*ousia*). See "**Substantial Being**"

Elements (*stoicheia*). Aristotle describes an element as "that out of which something is composed, as the first constituent not divisible in kind into a different kind" (*Metaphysics* V.3, 1014a26-27, tr. Joe Sachs). Some of his predecessors conceived this limit case to consist of particles that were the end-point of divisibility ("atoms", from Greek *a-tomon*, "in-divisible"). Aristotle understands the elements to be of two kinds: **formal** and **material**. Formal elements are indivisible because they are principles of ordered unity and wholeness; material elements (Earth, Air, Fire, Water, and "Aether", the material of the stars) are divisible, but only into more of the same (see **Material**). He is thus more in line with predecessors like Anaximander and the Pythagoreans, who understood Limit and the Unlimited as elements, and more tenuously Empedocles, who added principles of union and disunion (Love and Strife) to the more obviously material elements.

First Philosophy (*prote philosophia*). As the investigation of the first principles of being and intelligibility, what Aristotle calls "first philosophy" reflects upon the questions that all other kinds of philosophical inquiry ultimately lead the thinker to confront. He names and pursues such inquiry in his *Metaphysics*, whose title has subsequently become the name for this kind of inquiry.

Form (*eidos*). In Plato's works, *eidos* comes to mean the enduring and intelligible being of each kind of thing, that which **intellect** seeks to discern and speech to capture when we ask "What is it?" The outward manifestation of form enables us to recognize something as the **distinct being** that it is; but with greater discernment we see that the true form is the one "according to *logos*" (*Physics* II.3, 193a31) that constitutes the very articulation of that thing, its **being-what-it-is**. Ultimately, this articulation is a distinctly constituted kind of

being-at-work that is the **cause** and **governing principle** of the thing whose being and **attributes** it determines. In particular, each kind of being-at-work requires the appropriate **material** able to support its requisite **potency** (with the exception of the divine intellect described in *Metaphysics* XII.7). When the kind of thing in question belongs to the **category** of **substantial being**, the form is itself the substantial being of that thing in the most decisive and governing sense; and what Aristotle calls the thing's **being-fully-itself** is the active self-sustaining that is that thing's being-at-work as the form that it is.

Governing Principle (*arche*). "*Arche*" in common usage means a beginning, source, or ruling office. Aristotle describes its meaning more generally as "the first thing from which something is or comes to be or is known" (*Metaphysics* V.1, 1013a18-19, tr. Joe Sachs). Soul is more a governing principle of a living being than its **material** is (even though its material governs many of its **attributes**), because soul as **form** of **being-at-work** determines what material is necessary for its embodiment and enactment.

Imagination (*phantasia*). When we credit someone with imagination, we usually mean the ability to envision things that do not presently exist, and might or might not be possible. Aristotle uses "*phantasia*" to refer to the **potency** that provides the basis for doing this: the ability to present to ourselves images of what may or may not be present. If we stare at something attentively and then close our eyes and continue to envision it, we catch imagination at its root as the after-effect of the **being-at-work** of **perception** (III.3, 429a1-2). If we open our eyes and look at the thing again, it is some time before we can be sure whether we are seeing what is present to our senses or the image that was present to us in the absence of sensing. This introduces us to the various **affections** of imagination, such as retention, association, remembering and recollecting, all of which underlie the various ways imagination comes to be intricately entangled with our perceiving and thinking.

Incidental (*kata sumbebekos*). Aristotle distinguishes the attributes of a thing (*ta sumbebeka*, or what comes along with it) from the being of the thing, or *what* it is. The incidental is what is connected to a thing merely by happening to come along with it, with no strict connection to what it is. Having eyes with colored irises is an attribute that comes along with being human, but the color of any particular iris is merely incidental.

Intellect (*nous*). That by which a soul thinks and discerns the articulation of things (see *Logos*). Intellect is a **potency** of soul Aristotle is at some pains to distinguish from and relate to perception and imagination. His predecessors typically failed to do this, so that in their usage "*nous*" means something like what in modern English usage is called "consciousness". Thus when Aristotle is echoing this more careless lump-usage (usually in Book I), I have translated it as "mind", and when he uses it to distinguish the potency or act of thought, I have translated it "intellect".

Logos (plural: *logoi*). Most generally, *logos* means speech. It seems to derive from the verb *legein*, to gather. Speech gathers particular phenomena into words, and gathers words into discourse, and gathers the thoughts of speakers together in shared meaning; thus "word", "discourse", and "meaning" are all possible translations of *logos*. Speech presents phenomena in an articulated order, and so be-speaks an articulated order already in the things, so that *logos* can also refer (and in *On the Soul* usually does refer) to this inner order that articulate speech reflects; thus *logos* can mean "inner articulation" or "ratio" or "relation" (and at 403b1 Aristotle uses it as an equivalent for "**form**"). As the concentrated effort to communicate such inner articulation, *logos* can mean "measure" or "definition." It also names the human power to articulately apprehend the ordered being and relations of things ("reason") and to explain how and why such an apprehension is truthful ("argument").

Material (*hule*). Material is "that out of which something comes into being, still being present in it" (*Metaphysics* V.2, 1013a24-25, tr. Joe Sachs). It is always relative to the "something" in which it is present, the something that is defined by its **form**. Thus organs are the material of a living thing, which is what it is because of its form; but organs themselves are forms whose materials are tissues, and so on. Thus Aristotle says that form is prior to material, for we can only identify something as material in relation to the form it subserves. (See *Metaphysics* VII.3 for Aristotle's explanation of why the thought-experiment of understanding material on its own as the **substantial being** of a thing fails.) There is thus no concept in Aristotle's works that corresponds to "matter" in the sense of a distinct self-subsisting kind of being opposed to "spirit". Commentators sometimes distinguish "proximate material" (e.g. the organs as the immediate material of the organism) from other levels of material (e.g. the tissues or the **elements** of which they are composed as also material of the organism, but only transitively, through the intermediate levels of enmattered forms).

Mind (*nous*). See "**Intellect**"

Perception, Sense (*aisthesis*). Although contemporary usage often distinguishes between sensation and perception, either notionally or as distinct physiological stages (generally taking sensing as reception of raw data and perceiving as interpretive or organizing processing), Aristotle does not recognize such a distinction. *Aisthesis* is the apprehension of **forms** (or already-ordered qualities), received by contact or through a medium, from things that are present to the perceiver. In general, I have used "sense" and its derivatives when Aristotle refers to the five senses or distinguishes one of them, when he refers to the organs of sense, or when he distinguishes the three kinds of sensibles he treats of in II.6 or the "common faculty of sense" examined in III.2. I have used "perception" and related words when Aristotle refers to the general receptive **potency** of which the distinct senses are varieties, or when he refers to any **being-at-work** of this **potency**, or when he refers to all the senses as one class.

Potency, Potential (*dunamis*). In *On the Soul*, "*dunamis*" most often means a "potency", or an aspect of a thing's nature that is oriented toward a certain kind of **being-at-work**, and is set to work by meeting with its proper object or proper conditions. Thus the nutritive potency is set to work, properly speaking, by nutriment; the various perceptive potencies by their proper sensibles; the potency of movement by the desired object; and intellect by intelligibles. It can also mean "potential" in the sense of suitability to take on various **forms**: the bronze is potentially a statue, but also potentially a helmet. Thus we think of **material** as potential in relation to the forms it can take on. But when we come to contemplate living things, the line between the two senses of *dunamis* is hard to maintain: the body is only material for the living being inasmuch as it is organized to have the potencies of that being. In general, I have used "potency" when Aristotle is speaking of the different parts or powers of soul, and "potential" when he is emphasizing the state of not being at work.

Substantial Being (*ousia*). "*Ousia*" literally means "being-ness" and is the common word in Greek for property or estate, i.e. the kind of wealth (especially in land) that endures and remains the same, sometimes over generations, and provides the foundations of a family's livelihood and continued identity. Plato uses it to refer to the enduring being of a thing, the unity standing behind its changing appearances. Aristotle draws upon Plato's way of using it, but gives it two particular inflections. When he distinguishes the different ways in which we say that something "is" (or what he calls the "**categories**"), *ousia* is the one sense of "being" that underlies the possibility of other senses.

It is being as an independently standing thing of some kind, rather than as an **attribute** of things (quality, quantity, relation, position, etc., all of which have being in a derivative way). I have translated this sense of the word as "substantial being," both to emphasize the root notion of "being" and at the same time to recollect the traditional translation as "substance" and the association with the form of property that belongs to "a man of substance." It might also be translated "independent being" to distinguish it from the other categories of being, which all depend on it.

At other times, however, Aristotle uses the word less strictly, to refer to what it is that makes anything distinctly what it is and different from other things. In this sense he sometimes refers to items in categories other than *ousia* as having an *ousia* (for example, the "distinct being" of color, which is a quality rather than a substantial being). In general, in Book One where Aristotle is exploring what kind of inquiry he is engaged in, *ousia* means "distinct being" because he does not assume that the soul is a substantial being. In Book Two, chapter 1, he focuses explicitly on substantial being as a category of being and argues that soul belongs in this category.